THE OFFICIAL
HARVARD
STUDENT
AGENCIES

BARTENDING
COURSE

THE OFFICIAL HARVARD STUDENT AGENCIES

BARTENDING COURSE

third EDITION

HARVARD STUDENT AGENCIES, INC.
ALEXANDER Z. SPEIER, EDITOR

ILLUSTRATED BY AMANDA BURNHAM & PETER VANDERMARCK

St. Martin's Griffin
NEW YORK

THE OFFICIAL HARVARD STUDENT AGENCIES BARTENDING COURSE, THIRD EDITION. Copyright © 2000 by Harvard Student Agencies, Inc. All rights reserved. Printed in the United States of America. No part of this book may be used or reproduced in any manner whatsoever without written permission except in the case of brief quotations embodied in critical articles or reviews. For information, address St. Martin's Press, 175 Fifth Avenue, New York, NY 10010.

Design: Peter O. Vandermarck and Daniel O. Williams

Third St. Martin's Griffin Edition : December 1999
ISBN 0-312-25286-2

10 9 8 7 6 5 4 3 2 1

CONTENTS

HARVARD STUDENT AGENCIES
THE PRESIDENT IS NOBLE M. HANSEN III
THE GENERAL MANAGER IS ROBERT ROMBAUER

SPECIAL THANKS TO
ANNE CHISHOLM
BRIAN JOSEPH
JUSTIN KO
ANDREW MURPHY
C. REED LORENTZEN
MARVIN DANIELSON
This book is based on the course developed by Adam J. Tocci. Without his extensive work, the course and the book would not exist.

IT TOOK THOUSANDS, nay, millions of years for humankind to evolve to the point where its opposable thumbs allowed the species to finally achieve success in its tumultuous struggle to twist open a beer. And when this great triumph was achieved, there was much rejoicing, and much consumption of said beer...which might explain why the early clans of nomadic drinkers spent much time in their caves, hiding from the pounding sunlight, quivering in their intoxicated and subsequent hungover states. And in this darkness, it proved difficult for further evolution to transpire, for it was extremely difficult to successfully mix a drink in the absence of light. But lo—the noble clan of the bartenders emerged, and ushered in a new age of enlightenment and wisdom, vanquishing the beasts of ignorance with the bold proclamation, "A dry martini shall mix but a small dash of vermouth with a much, much larger quantity of gin." And thus was ushered in a new era, in which witticisms uttered from the sacred throne known as a bar stool be- came an acceptable substitute for work and productivity. And so did humankind demonstrate its gratitude by showering upon the bartender many tips and great affections, thereby making membership in the noble clan of the bartender appealing to all.

Because bartenders still occupy a much ballyhooed position in society, many people continue to seek the grail that is a Masters of Mixology. For too long, this quest has seemed distant and even impossible, a dream deferred for the easily dissuaded. This book, however, seeks to overcome that difficulty by demonstrating that the basics of bartending are easily learned. At a fundamental level, there is nothing complicated about bartending—the most crucial components are patience, practice, and persistence. Style and flair come with time, but bartending jobs and brilliantly orchestrated parties emerge out of a set of sound fundamentals that guides the expert production of tasty beverages.

For 25 years now, the Harvard Student Agencies Bartending Course has been turning amateur bartenders into an elite force of talented mixologists, spreading joy and well-prepared drinks throughout the world. Now, the accumulated wisdom of these decades squeezes itself into this book in hopes that you, dear reader, can enjoy the noble pursuit of the properly prepared drink and use it as a force for good, whether throwing the most brilliant of private parties or satisfying the most demanding patron at some watering hole. Along these lines, it bears mentioning that the techniques outlined in this book can serve as a point of departure into professional bartending, which is an excellent source of part-time jobs and spending money for college students or full-time work with fine pay in an extremely satisfying and very interactive line of duty.

At its core, bartending is a simple art, and this book is designed to show you the ropes as quickly and efficiently as possible. In Chapter One, you'll learn the basics about the organization of a bar, and the not so basics about the character of all of the liquid actors in the pageant of drinks. Chapter Two offers the supporting cast, detailing the technology and complementary flavors with which a bartender regularly works. Chapter Three examines the processes and recipes necessary to produce the most popular categories of mixed drinks. Chapter Four counters with the oft-overlooked world of beer, wine, and champagne, and some innovative uses for these staples of drinking culture. More unorthodox categories of drinks emerge in Chapter Five, offering some unusual and memorable varieties that will make a fantastic impression at any party; additionally, the chapter offers an arsenal of non-alcoholic drinks that is a crucial component of the good bartender's repertoire. Chapter Six offers some helpful hints to make sure that your private soirees run smoothly. Chapter Seven follows by examining how to make the jump into the professional ranks of bartenders. Finally, Chapter Eight offers some cautionary advice on alcohol's side effects and the responsibilities of the bartender.

"The Professor" wishes you best of luck with this Bartending book.

ON

SERMON

Aaaah, the noble six-pack. Long before the rift between its namesake Joe Sixpack and Champagne Charles fizzled into harmless quibbles over this or that quality of hops, and long before it was chic to cut the little plastic rings to prevent the slow suffocation of the oceans' population of sea bass or whatever, there was just the perfect amount of beer for one guy and the first half of a football game. We could count on the football advertisers to play to our most base desires, we could count on bikinis and wild beachside parties, a big bouncy ball, a friendly dog, turned-up "volleyball-style" sun visors, perhaps an improptu neighborhood car washing, and the guys. Yes, the friends, the buddies, your drinking pals. The stories you could tell, isn't that right Mr. Sixpack? When Spuds McKenzie, the trademarked dog of BadBoyz everywhere graced T-shirts and water-cooler conversations all the way from Houston to Lubbock. When guys could still know the value of a good cheap midday Hamm's buzz. And the land of sky blue waters, was a paradise for you and for me... But, I ask you, who out there likes the fancy beers, the microbrews, the little guys just trying to make it in this big crazy world. Goodness knows we want a special brew for each little area of our sainted country— from the graceful ski chalets of Stowe, Vermont, to the graceful ski chalets of Sun Valley, Idaho—there's a microbrew for every one of you connoisseurs, something fruity, something tangy, something with that little bit of punch you've been missing from those big American brews that are so full of big-budget media bluster and so lacking in the things a beer should be about...BIG BOLD TASTE! Certainly the microbrew revolution is no kind of scam to turn every good American into some kind of European beer fascist with the Upscale Tastes of the cognoscenti. Certainly there is nothing wrong with promoting the delicious tastes of a beer so charming that its name features a dirty pun, or evokes the sylvan beauty of... perhaps a ski chalet. So snuggle up with your buddies, drinking guys and gals of the future, and forget the revolution, listen to your Morning Edition and your Fresh Air, while you sip on something a little more civilized. But bartenders of the future, remember your heritage and your duty. Remember the love. Remember the trust. Remember the six pack.

✔ Peter Vandermarck

1

LIQUID TOOLS

GRENADINE AND LIME JUICE

THE CONTENTS OF liquor bottles often seem like the magical arsenal of a witch's brew. Confusion abounds among bartenders as to what, exactly, they're dumping into their delicious concoctions. Knowledge is power, however, and a basic sense of the subtle flavors that comprise a tasty mixed beverage can help to turn a babe in the bartending woods (it is, of course, illegal to hire infants as mixologists) into a certified escort into the world of liquid delectation. This chapter seeks to enable that transition, first by examining the basic setup of a bar and its correspondence to frequently ordered drinks, then by providing a sketch of the manifold flavors that comprise the masterful bartender's creative palette.

BASIC BAR SETUP

If you've ever looked closely at a professional bar or someone's well-stocked home bar, you've probably noticed that bottles are generally kept in two main areas: the "front bar" and the "back bar." A good bottle arrangement enables bartenders to make drinks efficiently, without having to search all over the place for the bottle that they need.

At the front bar, also known as the "well" or the "cocktail party bar," bartenders mix more than 70% of their drinks. As these names suggest, all the basic, most popular drinks can be made using the bottles located in this area.

A typical front bar setup is shown on page 10: vodka, gin, rum, tequila, and triple sec, from right to left—the light alcohols—go on your right. If you're serving drinks to a young crowd, you'll find that light alcohols are more popular than dark and should be placed according to your handedness: on the right for right-handed people and on the left for southpaws. This arrangement allows for slightly greater speed, which is a crucial component in bartending. On your left, from right to left, are whiskey, bourbon, Scotch, Rose's Lime Juice, and grenadine—the dark alcohols plus a couple of frequently used mixers. In the middle rest dry vermouth and sweet vermouth. The row of fancy bottles represents the "show row," which is found on some professional and large home bars. It is exactly the same as those behind it, except that each remains sealed and has the label facing the guests so that they can see which brands the bartender is pouring. The show row really doesn't have an official function other than to inform guests what is being served, and it is often omitted.

This setup, while common, is not absolute. Depending on the alcohol preferences of your guests, it is generally safe to say that the best setup involves placing the bottles that will be used with the most frequency within easy reach while not interrupting the normal order of the speed rail. For instance, add a bottle of coffee brandy to the end of the well on May Day, when a bunch of Commies will flood the bar begging for White Russians.

While there are occasionally variations on the basic ordering principle of the well, such anomalies are not frequent. Try to learn to work with the diagrammed order, but if you find yourself working in an establishment that follows different organizational principles, make sure that you learn them immediately—disrupting someone's setup can lead to disastrous outcomes, and a lot of very unpleasant drinks. The purpose of organizational consistency is to increase the efficiency with which you can serve drinks by placing the bottles in the same place every time so that you can grab them blindly.

In professional bars, a "speed rail" usually replaces the front bar. This rack, attached to the bar or sink directly in front of the bartender, holds "house brands" (usually less-expensive brands) of front-bar liquor. The bartender defers to the well brand of liquor for every drink unless the customer specifies a well-known brand, or "call brand," as it's known in bartending lingo. The more expensive call brands stay on the back bar. That means that you will prepare a White Russian with generic coffee brandy instead of the most commonly known call brand (Kahlúa) unless the drinker specifically requests otherwise (or if your bar is using Kahlúa as its well brand). There is one further classification of alcohols called the "premium" or "top-shelf" brands. These are even higher quality bottles of liquor—such as Bombay gin or Old Grand Dad bourbon—that cost even more than their counterparts. These bottles will also find a home on the back bar. There will generally be a list in the bars designating a price for each individual brand of alcohol.

The back bar, also called the "liqueur bar," contains liqueurs, brandies, and other less frequently ordered liquors. As the name suggests, bartenders usually keep those bottles behind them, since they rarely have to use these liquors and don't mind walking a few extra steps when they need them.

At first glance, the back bar appears to be a confusing array of bottles, apparently thrown onto the shelves in random order. Actually, the organization of the back bar follows two basic and sensible rules:

RULE 1: Keep bottles on the back bar separated by flavor base. For

CONTINUED IN THREE PAGES▶

YOUR BASIC BAR SETUP *

You may have read all about these things just a brief moment ago in the text, but this will remind you of what you've already read! It will also help visual learners catch up to all those textual learners for whom this whole two page spread is probably just incomprehensible squiggles and nonsense.

THE SHOW BOTTLES: Use these in fancy bars to show the customers what they're getting. Do not use in unfancy bars. Theoretically, they are the same brand as the one that's actually in your well, but this drawing is theoretically not theory-based.

GRENADINE:
Sweet and delicious! Used for Shirley Temples and Roy Rogerses.

LIME JUICE:
Always Rose's Lime juice. Why? People only deserve the best in lime juice.

SCOTCH:
Like blended whiskey, except grosser.

BOURBON:
Bourbon is perhaps the most delicious of the dark alcohols—a Maker's Mark and water will always hit the spot, no matter what the occasion or hour of the morning.

WHISKEY:
Keep the blended whiskey in the well, because it is the whiskey that tastes the worst.

SWEET VERMOUTH:
If you get the opportunity, you should see Dusan Makavejev's *Sweet Movie*. It will blow your mind. Sweet vermouth is used for martinis.

BARTENDER:
If this two-page pread were an actual bar setup, you would find yourself somewhere in the middle of the binding.

* WITH HELPFUL NOTES!

MORE SHOW BOTTLES: These are more show bottles.

DARK VERMOUTH: Used for the most masculine of drinks, the Manhattan.

TRIPLE SEC: A new addition to the modern 'tender's well. As it turns out, people like the way it tastes. Who doesn't love a good sidecar?

TEQUILA: Why is there a market today for high class tequilas? You might as well quaff a $1000 bottle of vintage grappa and drink your own urine.

RUM: The mis-understood booze with the carribbean flair.

GIN: Consistently the booze with the shortest, classiest name. Close finishers: rum.

VODKA: Here's an example of good vodka—Ketel One. Here's an example of what you keep in the well—Cossack's White Devil.

hint!

A MNEMONIC:
Can't remember the order of the booze in the well, try this poem:
vodka / ba bum! / gin / ba bum! / rum / ba bum! / tequila / ba bum! /
triple sec / ba bum! / from right to left / ba bum! / if you're a lefty /ba BAM! / reverse that. / yes!

CONTINUED FROM THREE PAGES AGO▶

example, put the four orange-flavored liqueurs together, the Kahlúa next to the coffee-flavored brandy, and all the call brands of Scotch near each other.

RULE 2: Keep bottles used for the same drink together whenever possible. For example, keep the brandy next to the crème de menthe so that you can quickly grab both of them to make a stinger. Chapter 3 will give you an idea of the more common liquor combinations.

MIXERS

Bartenders usually keep at least four carbonated mixers on the front bar. Cola and tonic water go best with light alcohols (as in rum and Coke or gin and tonic). Soda and ginger ale mix well with dark alcohols (as in Scotch and soda or bourbon and ginger). You might also want to have other carbonated mixers at the bar, such as 7-Up or Sprite, bitter lemon, sour mix, or any other of the many mixers available. Don't forget diet sodas; many people try to convince themselves that their drinks don't have that many calories by requesting diet sodas as mixers.

Bottled mixers will suffice for the home bar or for a small, relaxed corner pub; soda taps work well in medium-sized, moderately busy bars; but when dealing with large, crowded, high-pressure establishments, only a "soda gun" keeps the mixer flowing fast enough. Also known as an "arm" or a "snake," this dispenser consists of a long, flexible tube with a set of buttons on the end. Each button represents a mixer; the bartender merely pushes a button, and the desired soda gushes out of the gun. This device eliminates the inefficient hassle of searching all over the place for bottles, uncapping them, and running out every two minutes. If you work in a bar with a snake, ask the manager or a co-worker to show you how to set it up and make minor repairs. It's important to remember that there is a big difference between tonic water and soda water. Soda water (generally identified by an "S" button on the soda gun) is merely carbonated water—in its own right, it is flavorless, but it has some hyperactive carbon dioxide kicking around to give it "texture." Tonic water (generally noted with a "Q" on the soda gun, short-hand for quinine, an ingredient in tonic water), on the other hand, is carbonated, flavored water, generally resembling a slightly bitter lemon or lime taste that is softened by a small amount of sugar and all of its friendly bubbles. If you aren't using a soda gun, you can distinguish between the two waters by their labels—soda water has a blue label, while tonic water has a yellow label.

Juices, of course, also go well with many liquors. Some popular mixing juices are orange, grapefruit, pineapple, cranberry, and tomato.

There's no set order for how juices are kept at a bar, although it is important to know that they are kept in "juicers," instead of in clumsy cartons. Juicers are just containers with twist off tops that have attachable nozzles. They are referred to in the trade as "store and pours," since the speedpourer allows for easy pourin' of drinks, while the covers allow the juice to be stored overnight so that it doesn't turn rancid. Juices don't have a set order at the bar—you'll just have to identify the various beverages by their color (easily done for tomato, cranberry, and orange juices, but to distinguish between pineapple and grapefruit juice, you'll probably have to open up the juicer and sniff to clarify which is which).

Many drinks, such as Collinses, sours, and daiquiris, call for sour mix. This mixer contains lemon juice, sugar, and sometimes egg white to make the drink slightly foamy. Sour mix often comes in powdered form (Quik-Lem, for example); in a pinch you can substitute frozen lemonade mixed with half the prescribed water.

OTHER MIXERS INCLUDE:

ROSE'S LIME JUICE: A reconstituted lime juice used most often in gimlets. Rose's is sweetened, so do not substitute it in recipes calling for plain lime juice.

CREAM: Don't use anything heavier than light cream or half-and-half, or you'll fill the drinker's stomach too quickly.

MILK: For Sombreros, especially. It can be used as a substitute for cream.

WATER: To mix with whiskey. If your bar does not dispense water through a tap or a snake, keep water in a pitcher so that all the air will dissipate. Otherwise, drinks will appear cloudy from the tiny air bubbles in tap water.

ALCOHOL—PAST AND PRESENT

Even if you're aiming to become a professional bartender, it's not absolutely essential to know a great deal about the history and varieties of alcohol. The majority of bar patrons are unlikely to confront you with questions like, "Hey, barkeep, how many different varietals does the Sonoma Valley produce?" or, "Say, what exactly is the chemical composition of this Heineken?" Nevertheless, it's a good idea to have at least a little gratuitous historical and technical knowledge on the subject. In this section, we try to address relevant subjects (although we often wax irrelevant), starting with the chemical process that creates alcohol and moving on to a short history of alcohol in society, followed by brief explanations of the various kinds of alcoholic beverages. The discussion of the alcohols will follow the order of the speed rail in hopes of reinforcing the more edifying sections of this chapter.

CHEMICALLY SPEAKING...

Liquor contains ethyl alcohol (ethanol), as opposed to methyl (wood) or isopropyl (rubbing) alcohol. Of the three varieties, only ethyl alcohol is safe to drink. Ethanol forms as the product of a chemical reaction known as fermentation, in which yeast enzymes decompose carbohydrates into carbon dioxide (CO_2) and ethanol (C_2H_5OH). These carbohydrates come from either grain (in the case of beer and most spirits) or fruit, especially grapes (in the case of wine and some spirits). The carbon dioxide can be left in the alcohol, as in beer, or allowed to evaporate into the atmosphere. In a strange twist of affairs, ethanol is also used to make fuel for running cars; at the same time, it is used by drinkers as a fuel to disenable their ability to drive.

A VERY, VERY BRIEF HISTORY OF ALCOHOL

Civilization begins with distillation.
—William Faulkner

□ □ □ □ □ □ □ □ □
It should probably be noted that William Faulker, while being the author of some of the most beautiful pieces of fiction in the American canon, has given his name to a phrase every average American slangster should have at the ready: The Faulkner Flu—or waking up in morking with a groggy head and a sore throat from smoking cigarettes and drowning your muse in boxed wine.

Faulkner was technically wrong—distillation didn't really come into vogue until the Middle Ages—but his point was correct; historically, almost all of the world's great civilizations have consumed alcohol in some form. Since its use pre-dates written history, no one knows who invented alcohol. In all likelihood, nor did the grunting inventor, although it is likely that he or she quickly came up with a word (or moaning iteration) to deŝcribe the hangover that quickly followed. There is some evidence that early agricultural societies enjoyed a very primitive form of alcohol by chewing and spitting out grain to let the mixture ferment; enzymes in the saliva converted the grain starch into sugar and eventually alcohol. While this proved satisfactory to nomads who knew not the meaning of bathing, you probably don't want to try this at home.

More palatable concoctions were developed by

▶ CAVEMEN WERE PERHAPS DRINKING SOME KIND OF ALCOHOLIC BEVERAGE BACK IN THEIR CAVES, PERHAPS EVEN IN PLACES AS EXOTIC AS ASIA MINOR.

societies as far back as 10,000 years ago. At about that time, wine was first produced from grapes in Asia Minor. By 4000 B.C., the Mesopotamians and some Asian societies had discovered viniculture. By 1000 B.C., the Egyptians, Phoenicians, and Chinese had caught on. The Greeks picked up the art of winemaking from the Egyptians and passed it on to the Romans, who during their imperial reign spread it amply throughout Europe and every pore of their body, leaving them vastly too drunk to continue to rule. Early beer production developed concurrently; in the Egypt of the pharaohs, beer-making was entrusted to the temple priests, inaugurating a long-standing association of alcohol with religion and mysticism (such as the Christian act of communion). Throughout the world, the type of alcohol produced depended upon the available resources. For example, African societies used millet to produce beer, the Japanese fermented rice into sake, and viniculture thrived in the Mediterranean and anywhere else that grapes could grow successfully. The English made mead out of honey, while in other parts of Europe barley was used to cultivate beer.

To the would-be martini drinkers of earlier millennia, fermentation had one drawback—the process did not yield beverages with an alcohol content higher than 12%. Distillation, the process of altering a substance through heating, was known to the Greeks and others but was not widely practiced. Then, about a thousand years ago, the Scotch and Irish discovered that, by extracting much of the water from beer through distillation, they could produce a new, potent form of alcohol. They called it uisge beatha or usquebaugh, which evolved into today's word for whiskey. Throughout the British Isles, there was much rejoicing over this discovery, as toasts became more refined and hangovers became worse. ("Work," proclaimed Oscar Wilde, "is the curse of the drinking class.") Soon, alchemists all over Europe were experimenting with distillation and its products, affectionately known as aqua vitae, or "water of life" (not to be confused with Aquavit, a pernicious, herb-intensive, Swedish alcohol that is oft-described as liquid death). Early methods of distillation were rather crude, leaving a number of impurities in the liquor that they produced. it wasn't until the invention of the patent still in the early 19th century that it became possible to produce grain neutral spirits, from which most contemporary liquor is made.

Alcohol's position in modern life varies widely from country to country: the Bible, for example, contains a large number of references to the production and consumption of wine. European societies almost unanimously embrace alcohol consumption as an act of hospitality and sociability; this is also true in Japan. Muslim societies, however, frown upon the use of alcohol—its consumption is prohibited in the Koran, and in most Muslim nations it is illegal. Hindus take a less-prohibitive but still-negative attitude toward liquor.

In the United States, alcohol occupies a slightly ambivalent position. During Prohibition (1920-1933), the manufacture, sale, and distribution of alcohol was outlawed by the 18th Amendment of the Constitution. In political terms, Prohibition was a disaster—the use of alcohol by the public actually increased during this period, and poorly manufactured "moonshine" greatly increased the health risks associated with drinking. Prohibition is also widely blamed for the ascendancy of organized crime, as Beer Barons thrived on the vast black market created by the new laws. For drinkers, Prohibition brought with it a strangely exhilarating golden age of innovation, leading to the creation of a number of fine cocktails. Today, a variety of mostly Christian fundamentalist religious sects still proscribe the use of alcohol, and a number of "dry" counties in which it is illegal to sell alcohol still exists in some Southern states. That said, there is widespread acceptance of casual, controlled drinking, and scientific studies have now demonstrated that drinking in moderation—such as a daily glass of wine with dinner—can reduce the risk of various forms of heart disease. Aqua vitae indeed.

GIN

Deriving its name from the French genièvre, meaning "juniper berry," gin was originally prescribed as a diuretic. Although it has no officially sanctioned medicinal value today, some still swear that a couple of martinis can cure a wide variety of ailments. Of course, they generally die in very prompt fashion. Gin is known as "a drinker's drink," meaning a lot of people can't stand the taste of it...and those who do like it generally find that all liquors make a fine drinker's drink.

Gin production involves several steps. First, grains (often corn and rye) are distilled into neutral spirits in a patent still. This grain alcohol is then flavored with juniper berries and other botanicals, distilled again, and bottled at 80 to 100 proof.

Gin brands may vary because of the quality of the raw ingredients, the purity of the added water, and the recipe of flavorings added prior to the second distillation. If you plan to add mixers, subtle brand variations won't matter much, so buy a cheaper brand. After you buy gin, keep the cap on the bottle or it may spoil. After seven to 10 days without a cover, gin might taste milky; since it doesn't come from a mammal, that should provide some kind of instructive as to the need to throw away the bottle.

VODKA

Historians generally credit Poland with the invention of vodka, perhaps as early as the 10th century. Russians, as has so often been their historical wont, plundered the recipe from Poland and gave it its name: zhizennia voda, meaning "water of life." After experiencing a great deal of existential angst at the lack of originality imparted to this title, the Russians eventually shortened the word to its affectionate diminutive, vodka, which translates literally as "dear little water."

Vodka production involves three basic steps. First, fermented carbohydrates (usually grain) are distilled to at least 190 proof (dear big water) in a patent still. The grain neutral spirits are then diluted, or "cut," with distilled water to a range of 80-100 proof, and then filtered through charcoal to remove all distinctive character, aroma, and taste. This process makes it slightly more difficult to detect variations in quality among vodkas than other liquors. Nonetheless, brands of vodka still vary because of the quality of the raw materials, the purity of the distilled water added, and the extent of the neutrality achieved by the charcoal filtration. As with gin, if you plan to combine the vodka with mixers, you can probably get away with using cheaper brands, as the mixer masks the slight imperfections of the less-crafted product...unless you're drinking an atrocious brand that turns its consumers into fire-breathing demons.

A recent trend involves the flavoring of vodka. Vodka can be filtered through foreign juices to produce a distinct flavor, frequently a fruity one. This process is used in the creation of liquors such as Absolut Citron and other flavored vodkas. It should be mentioned that the flavoring process does not noticeably affect the alcohol content of the vodka; although the liquor might taste different, it is still as potent as the real McCoy.

RUM

Rum production involves the same basic steps used in making many other liquors: sugarcane juice and molasses (the carbohydrates) are fermented, distilled, sometimes aged, often blended, and then bottled at 80 to 151 proof. Because of variations in this process, you could perhaps find as many kinds of rum as there are brands, but most differ primarily by country of origin.

Puerto Rican rums such as Bacardi, the most common in America, are light-bodied and dry. They are fermented with a special cultured yeast, then distilled in modern patent stills to over 160 proof (fairly neutral), aged at least one year, and blended with other aged rums. Some Puerto Rican rums have an amber or dark color due to aging in charred oak barrels rather than the plain oak casks used for light rum. Virgin Island rums like Ron Virgin taste similar to Puerto Rican rum, but are slightly heavier and usually not aged.

Barbados rum such as Mount Gay also tastes heavier than Puerto Rican rum and has a darker color. Barbados rum is characterized by a soft, rather smoky flavor.

Jamaican rum such as Myers's is the darkest, richest variety. Whereas Puerto Rican production uses a cultured yeast, molasses for Jamaican rum is fermented naturally. Then it is distilled to less than 160 proof (which leaves some of the molasses flavor in the liquor), aged, often colored with caramel to darken the final product, and bottled at 80 to 100 proof.

Rums from other regions, such as Haiti (Rhum Barbancourt), Martinique, and New England (Caldwell's Newburyport) are much less common. All have their own unique characteristics.

Two other Puerto Rican rums merit special recognition. Some specialty drinks (Zombies, for example) call for 151-proof rum as an ingredient. Do not substitute 151-proof rum for regular bar rum (usually around 80 proof); it contains almost twice as much alcohol. On the other hand, spiced Puerto Rican rum, such as Captain Morgan's, can be used as a substitute for regular rums as requested by the drinker. It contains the same amount of alcohol, but with the addition of vanilla and other spices that impart more zest to the drink.

TEQUILA

Tequila is perhaps the most misunderstood of all liquors. Even some bar books still treat tequila as a mysterious Mexican potion full of worms, hallucinogens, and all manner of vile filth. In fact, tequila makers must adhere to strict government quality controls, which pretty much take all the mystery—and certainly all the hallucinogens—out of the liquor. Tequila must be made from blue agave plants (Tequilana weber, blue variety) grown in a specific, government-designated area of Mexico (an area that includes the town of Tequila). It must go through two distillations and contain at least 51% fermented agave juice.

Production of tequila involves basically the same steps as other distilled spirits: a mixture of at least 51% blue agave juice and up to 49% sugarcane juice (the carbohydrate) is fermented, distilled twice in pot stills, filtered through charcoal, and then either bottled or aged for one to seven years. Aged tequila, called anejo, may be stored in used oak barrels, which provide its golden color. Tequila is 80 proof in the U.S., 96 proof in Mexico.

You'll find worms only in mescal (and sometimes basketball uniforms), not tequila. Mescal is another Mexican liquor, similar to tequila, but it is not subject to the same quality controls. Mescal may contain other varieties of the agave from any area of Mexico. The mescal worm is harmless and, despite the innuendos of mescal advertisers, contains no psychoactive elements...unless it's one of those crazy worms that spends its free time consuming peyote (perhaps that's how it ended up in the bottom of the bottle). Originally, distillers probably put it there because the worm spends its entire life cycle in the agave plant, so providing it with a ceremonial burial in mescal seemed like a polite thing to do. Today, the worm in the mescal bottle represents tradition or a shameless sales tactic, depending upon your perspective.

WHISKEYS

Whiskey, whisky, Scotch, Irish, Canadian, bourbon, rye, blended, straight—whiskeys come in wide and occasionally confusing varieties. Most differ by country of origin, primary base grain, or variations in processing. Some are more or less interchangeable—as a bartender, you should know enough about the different varieties so that you can substitute them in drinks when necessary.

Whiskey production involves four steps: malting, fermenting, distilling, and aging. That last step imparts color to the whiskey; colorless alcohol goes into wooden barrels to age, and interaction between the wood and the liquor supplies flavor, aroma, and color to the whiskey. As soon as whiskey is bottled, the aging stops.

Whiskey or whisky? Which spelling is correct? If you look at a bottle of Four Roses (American), for example, you will see the word whiskey. But if you glance at a bottle of Chivas Regal (Scottish), whisky is emblazoned on the label. As a rule, Scottish and Canadian distillers spell the word without the e, and American and Irish whiskey producers include it.

The first qualitative difference is between straight and blended whiskeys. Some blended whiskeys contain mixtures of similar products made by different distillers at different times (as in Scotch); others have combinations of straight whiskeys and neutral, flavorless whiskeys (as in Canadian). Straight whiskeys, on the other hand, are not mixed at all, or are mixed only with whiskey from the same distillation period or distiller. The country of origin is a second important distinction. Scotch, Irish, Canadian, and American whiskeys are all made by different processes and, therefore, have very distinctive tastes.

Scotch, the whisky of Scotland, usually has barley (and sometimes corn) as its primary base grain. Scotch tastes smoky, a flavor it acquires when the barley malt roasts over open peat fires during the first step in production. Then this smoky-flavored malt is combined with water (the mash), fermented, distilled in a pot still, and aged at least three years in uncharred oak barrels or used sherry casks. All Scotches imported to the United States have been aged at least four years; the best ones are 12 years old. Most contain blends of whiskies and have been bottled at 80 to 86 proof.

Irish whiskey, which includes whiskey made in Northern Ireland, uses barley and other grains as its primary bases. Its ingredients and the methods used to make it are similar to those of Scotch. During Irish whiskey production, however, the malt roasts over coal-fired kilns, so Irish whiskey does not have Scotch's smoky flavor. Sometimes the

Irish blend their whiskies for a lighter product. It is then aged five to 10 years in used sherry casks and bottled at 86 proof.

American whiskeys include bourbon, rye, corn, bottled-in-bond, sour mash, and blended. Bourbon, named for Bourbon County, Kentucky, where this whiskey originates, is distilled from a fermented mash of at least 51% corn. The balance of the mash may contain any other grain, usually rye and barley. The aging process takes two to 12 years In oak barrels, after which the bourbon is bottled at 80 to 90 proof. Rye whiskey contains at least 51% rye grain in its mash. Real rye whiskey (such as Old Overholt) is not as popular as it once was, though, so it usually stays on the back bar. Be alert to this when worldly sophisticates order "rye and ginger," for example; they probably want blended whiskey (such as Seagram's 7 or VO). Odd as it may seem, a person who wants to drink real rye usually has to say so rather emphatically: "I want rye—I mean real rye, not that yuppie dishwater you're serving the kids." Corn whiskey is distilled from a fermented mash of grain containing at least 80% corn. Notice the difference between bourbon (51% corn) and corn whiskey (80%). In the U.S., bottled-in-bond whiskey is straight whiskey that was bottled at 100 proof and aged at least four years in U.S. government-bonded warehouses. Sour mashes contain some proportion of previously fermented yeast (as opposed to sweet mash, which is made only from fresh yeast). Jack Daniel's Tennessee Whiskey is made from a sour mash.

The difference between straight and blended American whiskeys may seem confounding. Straight means that the mash must contain at least 51% of a certain grain:

MASH	WHISKEY
51% barley	straight malt whiskey
51% rye	straight rye whiskey
51% corn	straight bourbon whiskey
80% corn	straight corn whiskey

Blended whiskeys are made from combinations of similar straight whiskeys from different distillations or distillers.

The choice of "the right whiskey" (or whisky) depends on your preferences. At a party, most hosts will provide at least two: Scotch and bourbon (and usually also a blended selection). Professional bars stock a variety of whiskeys (including at least three on the speed rail), so there you'll have a better chance of finding your favorite type and brand. Every brand whiskey varies in flavor according to its base grains, production techniques, and aging, so it is impossible to generalize about which is best. More expensive brands have probably been made with high-quality grains, careful production regulations (for a consistently

TOO MANY GRENADINES AND LIME JUICES!!!!

good whiskey), and longer aging periods. On the other hand, some expensive brands owe their premium price tags in part to having been heavily advertised so that people will pay for their image. Bars, of course, also charge more for these prestige brands.

BRANDY

*Claret is the liquor for boys; port for men; but he who
aspires to be a hero must drink brandy.*
—Samuel Johnson

While it is generally relegated to the world of after-dinner drinks (and hence absent on the speed rail), brandy is still a popular—or at least infamous—drink of aspiring sophisticates. In particular, it is associated with the ancient tradition of men adjourning for an after-dinner cigar and brandy. It is distilled from wine or a fermented fruit mash. If it is made from wine (that is, from grapes), the name brandy stands alone, but if it is distilled from another fruit, brandy is called by the fruit name. For example, apricot brandy contains an apricot base. Some brandies, however, have special names. Cognac, usually considered the finest of brandies, comes from the Cognac region of France. Armagnac, another fine brandy, comes from the Gers region of France. Metaxa is a sweet, dark, grape-based, Greek brandy. Ouzo, another Greek product is colorless and tastes like licorice. Calvados, an apple brandy from the Calvados region of France, is similar to applejack, and American apple brandy. Kirschwasser, or kirsch, is a clear, cherry brandy of European origin. Grappa is a dry, colorless, grape-based, Italian brandy.

LIQUEURS

Liqueurs (or cordials) were originally invented as aphrodisiacs; alas, like the worms in a bottle of tequila, this is a lot of nonsense. Today's liqueurs contain various plants, fruits, and other flavorings, and are often very colorful. All contain at least 2.5% sugar, but most have much more than that. In fact, the prefix crème de, as in crème de menthe and crème de cacao, refers to the high sugar content of the liqueurs, which gives them a creamy consistency.

Liqueurs of the same flavor base generally congregate on the back bar. To help you learn which ones taste similar, and can therefore be interchanged when necessary, the following list offers a partial grouping of common liqueurs according to flavor.

▶ **"WHAT'S IN THAT DRINK, FRIEND?"**
"WHY, PERNOD, MY GOOD FELLOW. THANK YOU FOR ASKING."

While admittedly incomplete, we've tried to include all of the variants of alcohol that you will encounter in the rest of the guide. New liqueurs and drinks, however, do not follow the guidelines that we've established, and a good bartender must needs stay atop current trends and new products. However, don't forget your most valuable gauge of new trends—the customer. If you keep your ear to the ground in a bar and try to learn the new-fangled recipes of the hipsters, everything should be peachy-keen.

▢ ▢ ▢ ▢ ▢ ▢ ▢ ▢
While your average run-of-the-mill hipster might ask for some kind of liqueur, the chic and the happening will more than likely get a gin and tonic or a manhattan.

NUTTY FLAVORS

Amaretto—almond

Crème de noyaux—almond

Crème d'almond—well, for obvious reasons, almond

Frangelico—hazelnut

Amaretto di Saronno is a high-quality, rather expensive, amber-colored liqueur, delicious on its own, in mixed drinks, and in coffee. You may substitute other brands to save money in some drinks, but choose carefully, as many do not taste the same as the original. Crème d'almond and crème de noyaux are similar; you can interchange these red liqueurs in mixed drinks if necessary.

Frangelico is a more infrequently used liqueur, and can't really be substituted for the other varieties, although it's every bit as tasty as these almondy flavors.

COFFEE

Kahlúa

Tia maria

Coffee brandy

You can sometimes interchange these and other similar products in mixed drinks, either to save money or when you've run out of something. People often order Kahlúa by name, but if they don't (in a drink such as a White Russian or Sombrero), use coffee brandy. Tia Maria contains Jamaican rum with coffee flavoring, and also provides a reasonable substitute for Kahlúa in a pinch.

BERRIES

Black Haus—blackberry

Boggs—cranberry

Chambord—black raspberry

Cranberria—cranberry

Crème de cassis—black currant

Maraschino—cherry

Sloe gin—sloe berry

Sloe gin, neither sloe nor gin, obtains its flavor from sloe berries, the fruit of the blackthorn bush. This red liqueur is popular in Sloe Gin Fizzes and Sloe Screws.

While very few people have ever heard of or cared about Black Haus, it is one of the tastiest varieties of schnapps that the hollowed halls of the Harvard Bartending School have ever dared to contain. And they have a very bizarre website (http://www.blackhaus.com).

FRUITS OF THE VINE

Cocoribe—coconut

Cointreau—orange

Crème de banane—banana

Curaçao—orange

Grand Marnier—orange

Malibu—coconut

Midori—melon

Peach schnapps—peach

Pisang Ambon—bitter orange

Triple sec—orange

The clear and bittersweet Cointreau and the orange-colored, cognac-based Grand Marnier are both name-brand orange liqueurs. Curaçao comes in both orange and a pretty blue. Make sure that you use orange when no color is specified, and blue when the recipe demands its use. Triple sec, a clear, tart liqueur, is not as sweet as curaçao. When a recipe calls for Cointreau, you can substitute triple sec if it proves to be more convenient or less expensive to use. Pisang Ambon is a green, bitter, orange-and-spice flavored, Dutch liqueur.

Many other melon liqueurs have appeared on the market in the wake of Midori's success. Taste them before trying to substitute, just to make sure that they're up to snuff; many aren't as good, but some will blend nicely in mixed drinks.

Cocoribe and Malibu are both coconut-flavored rums, occasionally used in tropical drinks.

HERBS AND SPICES AND OTHER SUCH VICES

Aquavit—caraway

Benedictine—mystery

Campari—bittersweet

Jägermeister—herbs and spices

Kümmel—caraway

Chartreuse—saffron or chlorophyll

Crème de menthe—mint

Crème de violette—violet

Crème Yvette—violet

Drambuie—honey

Parfait Amour—violet

Pimm's No. 1—herbs, spices, and fruits

Peppermint schnapps—mint

Benedictine and Chartreuse both date from the 16th century and contain exotic blends of many herbs and spices. Green Chartreuse is flavored with chlorophyll, while yellow Chartreuse contains a lighter and sweeter saffron flavor. Benedictine, produced by monks who will defend the honor and secrecy of their beverage by killing anyone who

▶ THE SAVVY 'TENDER KNOWS HIS LIQUEURS LIKE HE KNOWS EVERY NOOK AND CRANNY OF HIS NEW SPACE-AGE BACHELOR PAD.

pirates it, use a cognac base flavored with any number of mysterious herbs, spices, and fruit peels. Campari is a bittersweet, amber, Italian liqueur. Pimm's No. 1 contains herbs, spices, and various fruits in its blend. Jägermeister (literally: hunting master) contains a fully loaded blend of 56 herbs and spices, although it remains surprisingly sweet.

Aquavit and Kümmel are unique in that they are strong drinks that disgust many without even being elevated to the exclusive pantheon of "drinker's drinks." Kümmel is flavored with caraway, cumin, and fennel, while aquavit is made from potatoes and then flavored with caraway seeds.

Crème de menthe comes in two colors: green and white (clear). Many people drink it as an after-dinner cordial, or between courses of a meal as a palate cleanser. Consider color in deciding which crème de menthe to put in a drink. Fortuitously, many recipes specify a color.

The violet liqueurs (crème de violette, Crème Yvette, and Parfait Amour) are violet-flavored and -colored.

Drambuie is a honey- and herb-sweetened variety of Scotch.

LICORICE AND ANISE

Absinthe

Anisette

Galliano

Ouzo

Pernod

Sambuca

Absinthe contains a dangerous narcotic ingredient (wormwood) as well as a Herculean quantity of liquor (136 proof) and is illegal in the United States, although any number of blind, madder-than-hell French writers attest to the fact that it is not prohibited everywhere. Law-abiding residents of the U.S. use Pernod as a substitute. Some advice from someone who has sampled the bitter joy of absinthe: there are different ways to take your absinthe. Some strain it through sugar into a glass and then sip it up slowly. Others, and perhaps the more adventurous, know that absinthe is not only a mind-altering narcotic, but also an alcohol of very high proof. Thus, daredevils will put a shot of absinthe into a shot glass and light it on fire, finally sucking the vile liquid through specially-designed extra long straws. Absinthe supposedly will allow you to "see the world as you want it" after a shot, and "see the world as it really is" after two shots. However, after seven shots, you will feel like vomiting, and probably see the world like a retching sucker. Be warned.

Galliano, a golden, vanilla-licorice liqueur, comes in a very tall bottle and goes into drinks containing the word Golden, such as a Golden Dream or a Golden Cadillac.

CREAM

Bailey's Irish Cream

Belle Bonne

McGuire's Original Cream

Myers's Rum Cream

Toasted almond cream

Venetian Cream

Sweet cream liqueurs contain cream, alcohol, and flavorings. The alcohol preserves the cream so that the liqueur can be stored and served at any temperature. In a sense, these liqueurs are pre-mixed cream cocktails, so they usually contain relatively little alcohol.

2

TOYS & TRINKETS

TOYS & TRINKETS

IF YOU'VE NEVER worked at a fully stocked bar before, your first encounter with this vast world might be somewhat bewildering. No one led you to expect a brave, new, technological world that makes the special effects in Star Wars seem basic by comparison. Surely George Lucas would not dare be so bold as to produce the dizzying array of glasses or a bizarre appliance that looks like the result of an unholy matrimony of a Slinky and a spatula, unless he was seeking a new superweapon meant to annihilate the Ewoks.

Relax. None of these strange objects can hurt you, nor are they as complicated as they might seem at first glance. A few simple guidelines will allow you to master the different glasses in no time at all. And that funny-looking thing? It's a cocktail strainer. Perfectly harmless (unless you sympathize with the ice struggling to find its way into a drink; the ice deserves no sympathy).

In this chapter, we'll explain the various contraptions that keep things running smoothly at any bar, offering brief descriptions of the various utensils, glassware, and garnishes that you'll need to tend bar.

UTENSILS

Bartenders usually keep a variety of tools around to help them do everything from shaking to straining to pouring. The most basic and useful utensils comprise what we like to call the "bartending kit;" most bartenders would never try to work without them. (Blatant self-promotion—Order your own official Harvard Bartending Kit to be just like one of the pros! For more information, see the ad in this book.)

A basic kit contains:

-Shaker.-

SHAKER SET: Bartenders use a shaker to make whiskey sours, daiquiris, margaritas, and the other popular shaken drinks listed in Chapter 3. We prefer a steel shell for the outer part and a glass shaker that fits inside. Glass works best for the inner part because some recipes ask you to "eyeball" the right amount of liquor in a drink, and glass allows you to see how much you pour. Shakers come in many shapes and sizes; the Harvard Bartending Kit uses a 12 oz. shaker because it allows the bartender to prepare several servings of a drink at once. However, use what is comfortable for you and allows you to make drinks with the greatest speed and efficiency.

STRAINER: The strainer fits over the shaker so that you can pour the chilled drink into a glass without the ice cubes. This type of drink is referred to as "straight up," as in a martini straight up.

SPEEDPOURERS: Speedpourers fit into the mouth of a bottle and dispense the liquor at an even rate. As you will see in Chapter 3, these gadgets are essential for the speed-oriented bartender. Make sure to put the speedpourer in the bottle at a right angle to the label; with all the pourers facing the same way, you can quickly grab each bottle without having to check the direction of the stream of liquor. By positioning the bottles this way, customers are able to read the label as you pour, and it also ensures that the liquor flows at an even rate.

BAR SPOON: The recommended bar spoon looks like the one shown here, with a long, twirled handle and a small spoon at the end. This type of spoon serves three purposes: you can stir drinks with the handle, pour alcohol carefully down the twirled segment or onto the back of the spoon (when making layered shots, for example), and pick up fruit with the spoon. Although busy bartenders rarely follow the rule, the law in some states prohibits the handling of fruit garnishes, so the spoon is made for those bartenders who haven't gotten so big in their breeches that they think of themselves as "above the law."

COMBINATION CORKSCREW/BOTTLE OPENER/CAN OPENER: This tool proves to be highly efficient because three separate pieces can get lost too easily at a hectic bar. You should choose whatever feels most comfortable. If you have a pocketknife with 1800 gadgets, you can also amuse yourself amply if your shift turns dull.

JIGGER/PONY: The larger end is the jigger, which measures 1½ oz.; the smaller end is the pony, which measures 1 oz. Although sometimes quite handy, a jigger/pony or other measuring glass will become unnecessary after you're accustomed to using speedpourers. Some bars, however, insist that employees use measuring glasses to ensure that they don't pour too much and waste liquor. Additionally, greenhorn bartenders are advised to use the jigger and pony for a good little while to standardize their three-count (the three-count is discussed at greater length in "Measuring" on page 38).

The following items are also useful:

ICE BUCKET: Bucket, basin, bag, or whatever you have around for holding ice—anything clean is fine.

ICE SCOOP OR TONGS: They are nice for some occasions, though impractical in a busy bar.

KNIFE: You will need a knife to cup up fruit garnishes.

GLASSWARE

The following list (complete with illustrations) will familiarize you with some glassware options available in bars. For the home, purchase any or all of them. In a professional establishment, the manager usually decides which glass to use for each drink. These illustrations are merely examples of different types; you'll find many variations and creative adaptations from bar to bar. Be careful, however, and don't get too creative. Remember that the right glass makes quite a difference in the final appearance of a drink—wine loses some of its appeal in a beer mug (unless you're serving the wine out of a box), and a piña colada won't fit in a shot glass (assuming that your servings aren't ridiculously stingy).

HIGHBALL: Used for more drinks than any other glass (for all those gin and tonics, Scotch and waters, etc.), highballs vary considerably from bar to bar. Most are clear, tall glasses that hold between 8 and 12 oz.

LOWBALL: Also used for many drinks, lowball or "on-the-rocks" glasses come in different shapes and designs. Most hold 4 to 9 oz. and are best for drinks served on the rocks, such as a martini on the rocks, Scotch on the rocks, a Black Russian, and many others.

OLD FASHIONED: This 4 to 7 oz. glass looks similar to an on-the-rocks glass, but has a bump in the base to remind the bartender to prepare the sugar, water, and bitters mixture for an Old Fashioned. Today, many bars use these to double duty as on-the-rocks glasses.

COLLINS: Best for Collinses, sloe gin fizzes, and Singapore Slings, these 12 oz. glasses are frosted with some clear glass left at the top to remind the bartender to add soda water to the top of a Collins. They lend a cool, refreshing image to these drinks.

COCKTAIL/WHISKEY SOUR: Martinis, Manhattans, and other cocktails ordered straight up are initially prepared with ice and then strained into a 4 oz. cocktail glass. Sours are prepared in the same way and strained into a 4 oz. sour glass. The stem on these glasses enables the drinker to hold the glass without warming the chilled contents.

WINE: Wine glasses come in a wide array of shapes and sizes. Choose yours according to your own preferences.

SHERRY: Serve sherry, port, or apéritifs like Dubonnet in 2½ to3½ oz. glasses.

CHAMPAGNE: Champagne glasses come in two shapes and sizes. The American glass, by far the most popular here, is very wide and shallow and holds 4 to 6 oz. The European glass, tall and fluted, has a 7 to 11 oz. capacity for more hearty imbibing. The European glass is better for champagne than its American counterpart, and not just because it holds more volume. The tapered mouth of the European glass has less surface area, and thus holds the bubbles in longer (unlike the American glass, which allows the bubbles to dissipate quickly). Also, the European glass causes less spillage. Of course, what's a New Year's Eve without a few drinks spilled on you?

BEER: Usually holding about 10 oz., beer glasses come in two basic shapes—the mug and the Pilsner glass. Most people have already seen mugs. The Pilsner-style glass was invented for use with Pilsner beer (see page 96), but it is actually suitable for any kind of beer. Bar managers often prefer mugs because they do not break as easily as the Pilsners.

LIQUEUR: Also known as a "pony," this 1 oz. glass is appropriate for after-dinner liqueurs and layered shots.

SHOT: These 1 to 3 oz. glasses can be used to serve shots of liquor or to measure alcohol.

BRANDY: Brandy snifters range in capacity from 5 to 25 oz. All have basically the same shape, and are designed to be cupped by the hand to warm the brandy.

MISCELLANEOUS: The technology of containers can be as variegated as the drinks that fill them—coconut shells in Polynesian restaurants, free tumblers from the gas station, glasses with big mouse ears from that vacation in Orlando...The innovations never stop. In the absence of any receptacle, one can always drop a bottle into a paper bag and start swigging. Of course, such actions are not the ones that you will generally want to encourage as a bartender.

GARNISHES, GARBAGE, & ACCOUTREMENTS

Just as the right glassware can make a cocktail look infinitely more appealing, those additions the bartender puts in a drink can also make it look—and taste—better.

The words "garnish" and "garbage" refer to the fruits and vegetables that you drop in a drink. Although many bartenders use the two words interchangeably, they have different technical meanings. Garnishes change the taste of a drink, such as a lime wedge in a gin and tonic or a lemon twist in a bourbon. Garbage just makes the drink look pretty, such as a cherry in a Manhattan or an orange slice and pineapple chunk in a piña colada. Here are some garnishes and garbage commonly found on a bar.

LIME WEDGES: Cut the lime in half (through its equator) and then quarter each half, following the natural contours of the fruit, to make eight wedges. Squeeze the lime over the drink, rub it around the edge of the glass if you so desire, and drop it in. Lime wedges are popular

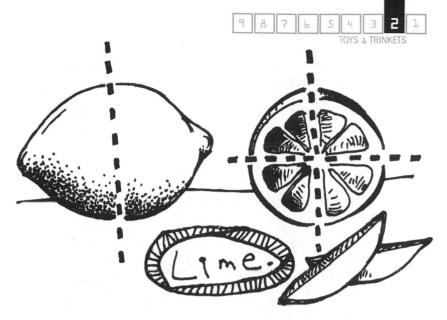

garnishes in many drinks, so keep plenty on hand. If you start to run low on limes, cut smaller wedges, but make sure you don't run out. Lime wheels: Starting at the stem, cut the lime in half. Lay each half with the flat side down, and cut width-wise to make semicircular, fan-like slices. Make a little cut down the middle of each slice so that you can slide it onto the rim of the glass.

LEMON TWISTS: Cut off the two ends of the lemon. Make a length-wise incision into the lemon's peel (between the two ends that you just cut off), then, with a spoon, separate the fruit from its peel. (You just use the peel in the drink.) Slice the peel lengthwise into ¼ in. wide strips. Twist the peel over the drink, rub it around the edge of the glass, drop it in, and stir. It's a good idea to keep some lemon slices or wedges at the bar, in case some fussy drinkers drop by who prefer a more lemony taste. Generally, you won't need to use too many lemon twists over the course of a night; cutting up one lemon peel at the beginning of the evening should do the trick.

ORANGE SLICES: Starting at the stem, cut the orange in half. Lay each half with the flat side down, and cut width-wise to make semicircular, fan-like slices. Make a little cut down the middle of each slice so that you can slide it onto the rim of the glass.

CHERRIES: Use stemmed maraschino cherries in your cocktails. Drinkers like stems, since they allow the cherry to be easily snapped out of the glass...and because they like to do tricks tying cherry stems in their mouths.

OLIVES: A must for the martini drinker, olives should be green, pitted, and without pimento.

ONIONS: Get little cocktail onions for your Gibsons—unless you don't know anyone who drinks Gibsons. Not many people do.

The wide variety of condiments and other flavorings in a well-stocked bar include:

SUGAR: Buy superfine, granulated sugar, which mixes more easily in drinks and won't leave a syrupy layer on the bottom of the glass.

SIMPLE SYRUP: An alternative to dry sugar. Some bartenders prefer to make simple syrup by mixing sugar and water together. Heat one pound of sugar in one quart of water until it dissolves. Keep it in a bottle with a speedpourer in it.

SALT: Keep a plate of rock, not table, salt on hand for making Salty Dogs and Margaritas.

GRENADINE: This red, non-alcoholic, sugar-and-pomegranate syrup colors and sweetens drinks.

BITTERS: As the name suggests, this mixer is bitter and infrequently used in drinks these days except in Old Fashioneds. You can add it to Manhattans or Bloody Marys if you like. Note that bitters is alcoholic and should not be used in non-alcoholic drinks, as even a few drops can be harmful to some non-drinkers.

BLOODY MARY CONDIMENTS: Keep any or all of the following on hand for Bloodies: Tabasco sauce, Worcestershire sauce, salt and pepper, horseradish, celery stalks. Some bars or servers like to keep a pre-fabbed Bloody Mary mix on hand to avoid the time-consuming hassle of preparing it when ordered.

Nutmeg: For Brandy Alexanders and eggnogs.

AND, OF COURSE, THE MOST IMPORTANT ADDITION: ICE...AND LOTS OF IT.

This rather extensive list of garnishes and condiments should give you an idea of the kinds of ingredients to expect in Chapter 3. Don't run out to the store and buy every one of them, however; just pick and choose according to your preferences.

ONWARD, FRIEND!

3

MASTERING MIXOLOGY

MASTERING MIXOLOGY

MOST BARTENDING GUIDES fall all over themselves trying to convince you that their book contains more drink recipes than the competition's. "Contains All the Drink Recipes Ever Invented!"..."Over 400,000 Recipes!" they proudly exclaim. Such claims hold only trivial merits, since you'll only really encounter about 50 or 100 of those thousands of wacky, wild recipes on a regular basis. More important is to learn the processes by which all of the drinks can be made, since you can always just ask a customer how, exactly, one concocts a "Tropical Wild Fuzzy Passionate Screw." Most drinks are so outlandish that customers will quickly retreat, changing their request to something a bit more manageable, such as a gin and tonic, while those who maintain a strong attachment to their obscure beverage will likely know the ingredients, having triumphed in their little game of "stump the bartender." Don't worry about memorizing these recipes unless your regular customers are ordering drinks with which you aren't familiar.

As luck would have it, most aspiring mixologists already have a pretty good grasp of the most important drinks that they'll need to learn how to make. Gin and tonic, Scotch and soda, rum and Coke, screwdriver...sound familiar? These drinks are basic highballs, which comprise at least 70% of all drinks a typical bartender serves. While some highballs might require a little extra effort, most are incredibly simple once you know the basic technique.

□□□□□□□□□

MEASURING

The following techniques provide relatively successful means of measuring alcohol into a drink.

n   Method 1: The Three Count—Fast as Carl Lewis and smooth as velour, the three-count technique provides the least cumbersome means of confronting alcohol measurement.   The

speedpourers (see page 20) that you stuff into a bottle's mouth allow alcohol to flow out at an even rate. If you grab the bottle by the neck, turn it completely upside down over the glass, and count to three at the right speed, you can measure out exactly 1½ oz. Get a bottle of colored water, put a speedpourer in it, and keep practicing until you get a cadence that measures exactly 1½ oz.,

or ½ oz. per count, into a jigger. Remember to grab the bottle firmly by the neck (place your index finger against the speedpourer for extra leverage, but be sure not to cover the air hole) for extra control. Practice repeatedly until you get it right. After a while, you won't even have to count anymore, as a three count will eventually feel right to you. Once you develop a good count,

you can use the cadence for all the other necessary quantities.

■   Method 2: The Two-Finger Technique—Put your two fingers together around the bottom of the highball glass and then pour in liquor until it reaches the top of your fingers. This method is faster than the jigger glass routine, but inaccurate rate; bartenders with bony fingers serve weak

HOW TO USE THE RECIPE GUIDE

Most of these recipes are categorized according to how they're made. This setup enables you to learn and remember the method at the same time that you see the actual recipe. If you want to make a specific drink, you can find it in the index. Below we have listed 12 main categories of drinks, divided into separate chapters according to the frequency with which you'll be asked to make these concoctions. The first three categories contain three subgroups: Basics, Populars, and Funs. Basic drinks are the old standbys, such as a gin and tonic in the highball section, martinis in the stirred section, and daiquiris in the shaken section. Popular drinks aren't quite as classic but do require memorization if you plan to work in a bar someday. Fun drinks include many you've never heard of before and may never need again, so you don't need to memorize them. Fun drinks are arranged alphabetically.

The 12 categories are:

CHAPTER 3: MASTERING MIXOLOGY

1. Highballs
   Basic (memorize)
   Popular (memorize if you plan to work in a bar)
   Fun drinks (no need to memorize—arranged alphabetically)
2. Stirred Cocktails
   Basic
   Popular
   Fun drinks
3. Shaken Cocktails
   Basic
   Popular
   Fun drinks
4. Blended Drinks

□ □ □ □ □ □ □ □ □

drinks while fat-fingered types will quickly become a drinker's best friend!

■ Method 3: Ride the Jigger, Not the Pony— Measure the liquor in a jigger and then pour it into the drink. This method is accurate, but too slow and cumbersome if you're working in a crowded bar. Some bar managers insist that their employees use this method to ensure that no liquor is wasted. If you must follow this procedure, here's a way to pour faster and make customers think they're getting a stronger drink. First, hold the jigger glass in one hand and the liquor bottle in the other. Pour less than 1½ oz. into the jigger glass, and then dump that into the highball glass while also pouring a little more liquor from the bottle. To the customers, it appears as though you gave them a full jigger plus another splash from the bottle in each drink. They will be pleased and probably tip you more. This is also a clever bit of deception to employ if a customer is complaining that her drinks are too weak.

HIGHBALLS

Highballs are defined technically as an iced drink containing liquor and water or a carbonated beverage and served in a tall glass. In the case of tending bar, however, usage defines a different, broader meaning, in which highballs are considered to be those drinks served on ice with any old kind of mixers that you can prepare directly in a 9 oz. highball glass (unless you prefer another, more creative presentation). Basic highballs are the most common ones you will serve, whether in a bar or at home. Fortuitously, they are also the easiest to make. Memorize them. It's easy—they are arranged by liquor to help you remember the ingredients. To make highballs, follow these easy steps:

1. Fill a highball glass two-thirds full with ice. Always do this using an ice scooper or your hands, never with the glass. For an explanation, read through "Scooping Ice," to my right, your left.

2. Pour in one jigger (1½ oz.) of liquor. Some bars prefer to save money by serving only 1 oz. highballs, however.

3. Pour mixer to the top. If you pour too little, it looks like you're skimping. If you are skimping, find a way to do so discretely. If you are caught, however, never lie about it while under oath to a grand jury—bartender's reputations can be impeached, too.

4. If the mixer is non-carbonated, stir it, or stick a straw in and let the drinker stir it. With carbonated mixers, do not stir. The bubbles do the mixing, and stirring tends to make the carbonation go flat.

5. Garnish the drink, if necessary.

SCOOPING ICE

NeverNeverEver scoop up ice with a glass; instead, always use either an ice scoop or your hand. Scooping ice with a glass is a big safety hazard, as a broken glass will seamlessly disappear into its icy counterpart. So dangerous is this frosty threat that state law often mandates the use of an ice scoop.

A bartending shortcut exists for producing several drinks at a time. It's fairly easy to do, but wholly unnecessary to learn unless you plan on working in a bar some day. If you want to make three gin and tonics, for example, follow these directions:

1. Line up three ice-filled glasses in a row with their rims touching.
2. Turn the gin bottle over the first glass for a three-count, then just move the bottle quickly over to the second glass and then the third.
3. Pour tonic in the three glasses.
4. Squeeze limes into the drinks.

The next time you go to a bar, watch the bartender and you'll learn other professional hints. Don't worry too much about exactitude—while you can't substitute whiskey for water or vodka for vermouth (unless you don't mind a quick slap in the face from an angry patron), the world will keep on turnin' even if you accidentally pour an extra half ounce of liquor into a drink. As evidence of this, notice how often recipes for the same drink differ from one bar book to another, or from one bar to the next. Hey man, this is bartending, and all truths are relative.

□ □ □ □ □ □ □ □ □
HIGHBALLS
Drinks with the word "highball" in their name, accordoing to common usage, contain ginger ale as a main ingredient. By this time, you know better—highballs are supposed to refer to a much broader classification of drinks (namely, all of the drinks listed in this section). Nevertheless, do not revel in your potential consumer's ignorance. Such an act is considered "impolite," and might mean that you have either your tip or this so-called "highball" thrown in your face.

BASIC HIGHBALLS

GIN

GIN AND TONIC
1½ oz. gin
tonic to fill
Garnish with a lime wedge.

GIN HIGHBALL
1½ oz. gin
ginger ale to fill
Garnish with a lemon twist.

SODA WATER

Soda and tonic water are not easily confused with wine. Just in case you need a refresher, these two mixers are generally carbonated, wine generally is not. Many beginning bartenders seem hell-bent on minimizing this fundamental distinction, however, as they let their giant bottles of soda water and tonic water breathe. But vicious irony of ironies, tonic and soda water, when left to breathe, quickly die, going flat and with exceptional speed once opened. Do not be victimized by the short lifespan of carbonation! Always re-cap your bottles, put them in the refrigerator when you're not using them, and buy smaller bottles if you're not serving large numbers of people.

GIN BUCK

1½ oz. gin

juice of ½ lemon

ginger ale to fill

GIN RICKEY

1½ oz. gin

soda water to fill

Garnish with a lemon twist.

This is the only gin and clear mixer garnished with a lemon twist—most call for a lime wedge.

GIN AND ORANGE JUICE

1½ oz. gin

orange juice to fill

This drink is fairly self-explanatory, although some folks try to make it a more nuanced experience by referring to it as a "left-handed screwdriver."

GREYHOUND

1½ oz. gin

grapefruit juice to fill

Again, beware the intricacies of the drinker's vocabulary. To avoid confusion, many people will simply ask for a gin and orange juice when they desire this specific recipe. Blessed are they. However, when invoking the term "greyhound," many drinkers want vodka as the main ingredient when hoping to experience this fast, smooth puppy.

SALTY DOG

1½ oz. gin

grapefruit juice to fill

Pour this drink into a highball glass rimmed with salt. Vodka is sometimes substituted for gin in this drink—always ask a drinker which breed of dog they prefer. This one is easy to remember, as it's merely a greyhound with a salted glass. (See sidebar on the next page)

VODKA

VODKA AND TONIC

1½ oz. vodka

tonic water to fill
Garnish with a lime wedge.

VODKA HIGHBALL

1½ oz. vodka

ginger ale to fill

Garnish with a lime wedge.

SCREWDRIVER

1½ oz. vodka

orange juice to fill

CAPE CODDER

1½ oz. vodka

cranberry juice to fill

Garnish with a lime wedge.

MADRAS

1½ oz. vodka

orange juice to ¾ fill

cranberry juice to fill

Dribble cranberry juice around the top to give a blotchy appearance. Don't stir. This drink might remind you of a bright madras plaid.

SEABREEZE

1½ oz. vodka

grapefruit juice to ¾ fill

cranberry juice to fill

Stir. This drink is a pretty pink color.

VODKA "7"

1½ oz. vodka

7-Up, Sprite, or any lemon-lime soda to fill

Garnish with a cherry and an orange slice.

BLOODY MARY

1½ oz. vodka

tomato juice to ¾ fill

small splash lemon juice

dash Worcestershire sauce

dash Tabasco sauce (more for a hotter drink)

shake of salt and pepper

¼ tsp. horseradish (optional)

DRINK CONTINUED ON THE NEXT PAGE▶

□□□□□□□□□
SALTING EDGES

Rimming your glass with salt is a lot easier than trying to garnish a small yet ferocious animal. The following three easy steps should provide for a successfully salted drinking vessel:
1) Pour rock salt on a plate. Kosher Salt generally works best, as its crystals are bigger and cling to the glass with much greater ease.
2) Rub a lime wedge around the rim of the glass.
3) Roll the rim of the glass around in salt.

□□□□□□□□□
MNEMONICS

Many aspiring bartenders are afflicted with heart palpitations when confronted with the seemingly limitless domain of alcoholic delights. Fortunately for those of you who have devoted a lifetime to memorizing the statistics of the '61 Yankees, we've come up with any number of mnemonic devices geared toward helping you preserve cherished cranial capacity for generally irrelevant information. If you can't remember that cranberries grow on Cape Cod, Massachusetts, try to try to learn alliterative linkages— Cape Codder and cranberry juice sure do have a bunch of C's!

THE BLOODY MARY

"Bloody" drinkers have diverse tastes, so you should ask if the drinker would like the drink hot, and then alter accordingly with Tabasco sauce. There are about as many different recipes for Bloody Marys as there are drinkers. Some prefer gin to vodka, and any number of interesting ingredients may be added or substituted to make that perfect, customized Bloody Mary. You can experiment with clam juice, dill, basil, garlic, curry powder, or barbecue sauce (yee-haw!). Feel free to be creative; you may be the bartender who discovers the perfect combination!

Shake all of these ingredients with ice, then strain into a glass filled with ice. Garnish with a lime or (for the more ambitious and vegetably inclined) a celery stick.

RUM

RUM AND TONIC

1½ oz. rum

tonic water to fill

Garnish with a lime wedge.

RUM AND COKE

1½ oz. rum

cola (or diet cola) to fill

CUBA LIBRE

1½ oz. rum

cola to fill

Garnish with a lime wedge.

Cuba Libre ("free Cuba") is just a fancy name for a rum and cola with a lime wedge, although to true revolutionaries, it has a much stronger meaning and is often accompanied by the singing of one anthem or another. Nuts to Castro!

RUM HIGHBALL

1½ oz. rum

ginger ale to fill

Garnish with a lemon twist.

Soda water can be substituted for ginger ale in this variation on a "highball."

RUM AND ORANGE JUICE

1½ oz. light rum

orange juice to fill

This drink is sometimes called a rum screwdriver.

RUM AND PINEAPPLE JUICE

1½ oz. rum

pineapple juice to fill

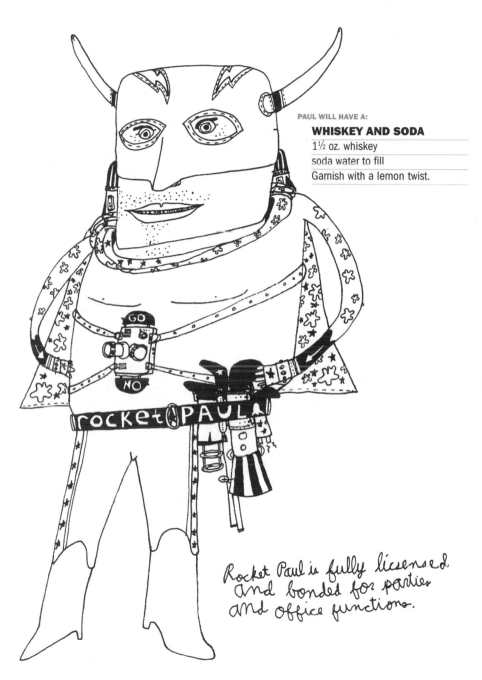

PAUL WILL HAVE A:

WHISKEY AND SODA

1½ oz. whiskey

soda water to fill

Garnish with a lemon twist.

Rocket Paul is fully licensed and bonded for parties and office functions.

RUM COOLER

1½ oz. rum

7-Up, Sprite, or soda water to fill

Garnish with a lemon wedge.

WHISKEY

The following highballs can contain bourbon, blended whiskey, Scotch, or some other whiskey. The drinker will tell the bartender what to put in—Scotch and water, for instance. Often with these dark alcohols, drinkers prefer to choose a brand, such as a Dewar's and soda instead of just Scotch and soda.

Dealing with the many different kinds of whiskey often frustrates and confuses new bartenders, or even a drinker of light alcohols for that matter. If you fit into either of these categories, read over the whiskey section of Chapter 1 before trying to serve these drinks.

□ □ □ □ □ □ □ □ □
WHISKEY

Some whiskey drinkers belong to the very devout kingdom of straight Scotch. Do not cross these people; follow their instructions rigorously. They'll often order a Scotch on the rocks or blended whiskey with just a splash of water. Some will request a brand, such as "J&B neat" (remember that "neat" means straight out of the bottle with no ice). Serve these drinks in rocks glasses. The garnish for dark alcohols is usually a lemon twist, both for lowballs (rocks) and highballs. With sweet mixers, leave out the twist.

WHISKEY AND WATER

1½ oz. whiskey

water to fill

Garnish with a lemon twist. Some people request only a splash of water. A splash equals ½ oz., so just put a little water in (no need to measure) and serve it in a rocks glass.

WHISKEY AND SODA

1½ oz. whiskey

soda water to fill

Garnish with a lemon twist.

HIGHBALL

1½ oz. whiskey

ginger ale to fill

PRESBYTERIAN

1½ oz. whiskey (usually blended)

equal parts soda water and ginger ale to fill

This drink is often called a "Press" or a "VO Press." The latter contains Seagram's VO whiskey, a name brand. If you don't have VO, suggest another blended whiskey as a substitute.

SEVEN AND SEVEN

1½ oz. Seagram's 7
7-Up to fill
Garnish with a lemon.

This drink requires name-brand whiskey and the right mixer. If you are missing either ingredient, suggest substitutes. However, be sure to let the drinker know you are substituting ingredients.

POPULAR HIGHBALLS

The popular-drink section contains recipes that are either simple variations of the basics or more complicated, yet often ordered, drinks. If you plan to work at a bar, memorize these recipes. They are arranged by liquor type (and, within these, by variations) to make it easier for you to remember ingredients and proportions.

VODKA AND APPLE JUICE (OR LEMONADE)

1½ oz. vodka
apple juice or lemonade to fill

HAWAIIAN SEABREEZE

1¼ oz. vodka
equal amounts of pineapple juice and cranberry juice to fill

This drink is delightfully easy to remember if referred to as a "Hawaiian Seabreeze," as it merely substitutes a little touch of Hawaii (pineapple juice) for the grapefruit juice in a normal Seabreeze. Unfortunately, local conventions provide for ample possible confusion, as the drink sometimes goes undercover as a "Downeaster" or a "Bay Breeze."

FUZZY NAVEL

1 oz. peach schnapps
1 oz. vodka
orange juice to fill
Garnish with an orange.

Sometimes an extra ounce of peach schnapps is substituted for the vodka.

DRINKS CONTINUED IN THREE PAGES▶

TAKE A BREAK

HOW DOES YOUR HEAD FEEL NOW? IF YOU'RE AT ALL LIKE ME, YOUR HEAD IS TELLING YOU IT JUST CAN'T HANDLE ALL THIS INFORMATION...

FROM ALL THIS

...LIKE WHICH VERMOUTH GOES WITH WHAT KIND OF ALCO-HOL? AIEEEEE!!!!!! AFTER A WHILE, SOME PEOPLE ARE JUST READY TO SNAP...

HARD LEARNIN'

...THEY JUST SAY "TO HECK WITH 'TENDING, THIS ISN'T MY BAG!" WELL, BY PAGE 48 OF THIS GUIDE, YOU SHOULD STOP CLUTCHING YOUR BLEEDING SKULL...

AND JOIN US

...AND REMEMBER THAT A GOOD BARTENDER NEED NOT BE SOME KIND OF ALBERT EINSTEIN OR LIKE A BRAIN SURGEON OR A ROCKET SCIENTIST...

IN A SIMPLE

...OR LIKE MARIE CURIE OR LINUS PAULING. BEING A GOOD BARTENDER IS LIKE PLAYING TIC-TAC-TOE WITH AN INFANT...

GAME OF WITS...

...sometimes the infant will get a game or two from you, but more often than not, the infant will not be able to understand the rules, and you'll be able to take it every time. sometimes things get like that...

**OK. GO TO THE NEXT PAGE, AND TRY TO WIN IN
ONE MOVE... YOU'RE UP. YOU'RE X.**

1. THE FIRST FEW ARE SOME EASY ONES:

2. AFTER FOUR GAMES, MOST INFANTS STILL HAVEN'T CAUGHT ON:

3. BUT AFTER EIGHT GAMES, YOU MIGHT EXPECT TO DROP A COUPLE:

4. TWELVE GAMES IN, YOU'LL LEARN WHAT THE GAME IS TRULY ABOUT:

SPACE-CHILD,

5. CAN YOU SEE IT NOW? ARE YOU TRULY FREE?

WELL, THE REST OF THE BOOK SHOULD BE NO SWEAT AT ALL.

SEX ON THE BEACH

1½ oz. vodka

1 oz. peach schnapps

cranberry juice to ¾ full

orange juice to fill

Serve with ice in a highball glass. Garnish with orange or pineapple.

SLEAZY SEX ON THE BEACH

1½ oz. vodka

1 oz. Grand Marnier

cranberry juice to ¾ full

orange juice to fill

Serve with ice in a highball glass.

MOSCOW MULE

1½ oz. vodka

ginger beer to fill

Garnish with a lime wedge.

This beverage is traditionally served in a coffee or copper mug.

MIND ERASER

1½ oz. Kahlúa

1½ oz. vodka

soda water to fill

Pour over ice in a highball glass and serve with a straw. Do not shake or stir, since the layering of ingredients is part of the effect. The drinker finishes it off like a shot "down in one" through a straw.

HARVEY WALLBANGER

1½ oz. vodka

orange juice (fill almost to top)

1 oz. Galliano (float on top)

This is a screwdriver with Galliano on top.

KOOLAID

1 oz. vodka

1 oz. Southern Comfort

1 oz. amaretto

1 oz. Midori
cranberry juice to fill

Serve with ice in a highball glass.

PURPLE HAZE

1½ oz. vodka

1½ oz. Chambord

1 oz. triple sec

splash of lime juice

soda water to fill

Serve over ice in a highball glass. Like a Mind Eraser, this drink is served in a highball glass, but the drinker finishes it off "down in one" through a straw before excusing himself while he kisses the sky.

BULLDOG HIGHBALL

1½ oz. gin

ginger ale to ¾ fill

orange juice to fill

This is a gin highball with some orange juice in it.

RUM CAPE CODDER

1½ oz. rum

cranberry juice to fill

Just substitute rum for the vodka in a Cape Codder.

TEQUILA SUNRISE

1½ oz. tequila

orange juice to fill

splash (½ oz.) of grenadine

Make this like a tequila screwdriver and stir. Then, gently add the grenadine to the top of the drink to achieve the "sunrise" look.

TEQUILA SUNSET

1½ oz. clear tequila

dash lime juice

orange juice

Stir, then float ½ oz. blackberry brandy on top.

MEXICOLA

1½ oz. tequila

cola to fill

Garnish with a lime wedge.

This is a tequila version of the Cuba Libre. Drinkers call this by other names, such as tequila and cola. However, the references to Mexico in a drink name generally indicates the presence of tequila.

BLOODY MARIA

1½ oz. tequila

tomato juice to ¾ fill

small splash lemon juice (or garnish with a lemon slice or lime wedge)

dash Worcestershire sauce

dash Tabasco sauce (more for a hotter drink)

a shake of salt and pepper

¼ tsp. horseradish (optional)

Garnish with a lime or celery stick. Ask if the drinker would like the drink hot, and then adjust the Tabasco accordingly. This drink is a Bloody Mary with tequila instead of vodka.

FREDDY FUDPUCKER

1½ oz. tequila

orange juice (fill almost to top)

1 oz. Galliano (float on top)

This drink is a tequila version of the Harvey Wallbanger.

LONG ISLAND ICED TEA

1 oz. gin

1 oz. vodka

1 oz. rum

1 oz. tequila

1 oz. triple sec (optional)

splash sour mix

splash Rose's lime juice

cola to fill (after stirring)

Iced Teas are very popular these days. If made correctly, they taste like real iced teas (inexplicably, given the actual absence of this ingredient), but feel very different when you find out that all of those lonely ounces can add up to a can of whoop-ass opened on your drunken self. In states with stringent alcohol laws, drinks with 4 oz. (the amount found in Iced Teas) of hard alcohol are prohibited. As a result, bartenders will frequently reduce the presence of each individual alcohol to ½ oz.

SLOE DRIVER

1½ oz. sloe gin

orange juice to fill

comfortable screw

1½ oz. Southern Comfort

orange juice to fill

SLOE SCREW

1½ oz. vodka

1 oz. sloe gin

orange juice to fill

SLOE COMFORTABLE SCREW

1½ oz. vodka

1 oz. sloe gin

1 oz. Southern Comfort

orange juice to fill

SLOE COMFORTABLE SCREW UP AGAINST THE WALL

1½ oz. vodka

1 oz. sloe gin

1 oz. Southern Comfort

orange juice (almost to fill)

1 oz. Galliano (float on top)

SCREW-UP

1½ oz. vodka

splash orange juice

7-Up, Sprite, or other lemon-lime concoction to fill

Garnish with an orange.

MEXICAN SCREW

2 oz. tequila

orange juice to fill

Garnish with the states of Texas, California, and an orange.

□□□□□□□□

SLOES & SCREWS

The following seven drinks are grouped together to illustrate a helpful technique for drink memorization. They are all modifications of a screwdriver, and while many drinkers will order them solely for the sake of a few sophomoric giggles, a bartender need not be offended by the absurdity of having a patron approach them by saying, "I'd like a Sloe Comfortable Screw...please." Instead, savvy servers will content themselves to know that a) the person ordering the drink will go home lonely, and b) the drink's name clarifies all of its ingredients. Because so many drinks are simple variations on each other, look for key words in the name of the drink that give away the ingredients. A Sloe Comfortable Screw Up Against the Wall is a complicated drink with many ingredients; however, by dissecting the title any rookie bartender should be able to make it: Sloe (sloe gin) Comfortable (Southern Comfort) Screw (vodka and orange juice) Up Against the Wall (Galliano—as in Harvey WALLbanger).

FUN HIGHBALLS

You don't have to memorize these drinks because they aren't ordered too often, but keep this book at the bar just in case. They are listed alphabetically for easy reference.

AMARETTO, ORANGE JUICE, AND SODA

1½ oz. amaretto

equal parts orange juice and soda to fill

Garnish with an orange slice.

BULLDOG

1 oz. vodka or rum

1 oz. Kahlúa

cream to fill

Top with a splash of cola.

CALIFORNIA ROOT BEER

1½ oz. Kahlúa

1 oz. Galliano

Stir in a highball glass and fill with root beer.

DARK AND STORMY

1½ oz. dark rum

ginger beer to fill

This delicious drink is popular in Bermuda, where they use Gosling's rum. If you can't find Gosling's, use another dark or spiced rum.

GENTLE BEN

¾ oz. vodka

¾ oz. gin

¾ oz. tequila

orange juice to fill

Garnish with a cherry and an orange slice.

KAHLÚA AND ICED COFFEE

1½ oz. Kahlúa

iced black coffee to fill

KAHLÚA ROOT BEER FLOAT

1 oz. Kahlúa

1 oz. root beer

dash Galliano

club soda to fill

top with a scoop of vanilla ice cream

Do not serve on ice.

KAHLÚA, RUM, AND SODA
1½ oz. Kahlúa
1 oz. rum
soda to fill

LIME RICKEY
1½ oz. gin
½ oz. Rose's lime juice
soda water to fill

MOJITO
1½ oz. light rum
1 tsp. sugar
dash Rose's lime juice

Stir vigorously in a glass with ice, then fill with soda water. Garnish with lemon slice and mint.

ORIENTAL RUG
1 oz. Kahlúa
1 oz. Bailey's Irish Cream
1 oz. Frangelico
1 oz. Jägermeister
cola to fill

Serve over ice in a highball glass. The many swirling colors provide this drink with its name.

RECEPTACLE
1½ oz. vodka
splash each: orange, pineapple, cranberry juices
top with 7-Up or Sprite
Garnish with a cherry and an orange slice.

RED DEATH
½ oz. vodka
½ oz. sloe gin
½ oz. Southern Comfort
½ oz. amaretto
½ oz. triple sec
½ oz. lime juice
½ oz. orange juice

Stir and serve over ice. Add enough grenadine for a deep red color. This nasty concoction can also be served as a shot.

REN AND STIMPY

1½ oz. gin

1½ oz. Chambord

cola to fill

Garnish with a lime wedge and serve over ice in a highball glass.

TEQUILA DREAM

1½ oz. tequila

splash cranberry juice

iced tea to fill

Garnish with lime.

This drink harbors no similarities to the "Tequila Mockingbird" depicted in the shaken section, with the single exception that one disgruntled student (and, arguably, his roommate) thought that in mixing these elements together, he had come up with a tasty concoction deserving of a clever name—namely, that of a "Tequila Mockingbird." Upon discovering that the name had already been taken, his hopes were shattered, leading him to impart a subtle hint of tragedy into his drink's moniker.

WATERMELON

1 oz. strawberry liqueur

1 oz. vodka

orange juice to ¾ full

sour mix to fill

dash of grenadine

Serve over ice in a highball glass. Garnish with an orange slice.

STIRRED COCKTAILS

The stirred cocktail category includes drinks such as martinis, Manhattans, and gimlets. They are stronger than highballs and measure about 3 oz. of liquid. The exact amount of liquid in the drink depends on the size of the serving glass. Just remember to keep the proportions the same as those listed in these recipes, and don't be afraid to eyeball it if you need to.

You can make stirred cocktails two ways: straight up (or just "up") or on the rocks (or just "rocks"). Straight-up cocktails are made in a shaker glass with ice and then strained into a cocktail glass without ice. On-the-rocks drinks can be made either right in a rocks glass with ice or stirred in a shaker and then strained into a glass with fresh ice. Ask if the drinker prefers a "rocks" or "up" drink, and then:

1. Fill a 12 oz. shaker glass two-thirds full with ice.
2. Put the smallest ingredient in first until all ingredients are in the shaker. It's important to put in the less substantial ingredient first (in the case of a martini, the vermouth) so that you can always adjust in case you pour too much. If you put the gin into a martini before adding too much vermouth, you have to throw the whole drink away. Haste makes waste!
3. Stir well. Very well.
4. Strain the drink into a serving glass.
5. Garnish, if necessary.
basic stirred cocktails
Memorize these classics and practice making them, as martini drinkers are the fussiest people in the world. Be prepared.

MARTINIS

Time to slip out of these wet clothes and into a dry martini.
—Mae West

Martinis are one of the more under-appreciated arts of the modern world. Figuring out how to pour in the right amount of vermouth is a struggle even for superstar bartenders. If you are using a metal shaker for your martini—like the pros do—some suggest that the ideal way to measure out the vermouth in a martini is by rimming the full edge of the shaker with the stuff. For a dry martini, these experts claim that rimming half the edge of the shaker will do the trick. For an extra dry martini, a drinker wants naught but a hint of vermouth, which amounts to splashing a little bit of vermouth in the empty shaker, swirling it around, then emptying it out before stirring the gin and ice.

MARTINI

1 part dry vermouth

5 parts gin

Pour just a small splash of vermouth (about a one count or a shaker's circumference) in the shaker and then a five count (2½ oz.) of gin. Melted ice will bring the liquid content up to 3 oz. Garnish with two olives (pitted and without pimentos).

□ □ □ □ □ □ □ □

"MARTINIS"

In recent years, as the popularity of martinis has swelled to ridiculous heights not seen since the dream-like days of the "three-martini lunch" (thank you, Jimmy Carter), a number of off-shoot, pseudo-martinis have arisen. Many of these new-fangled drinks have no resemblance to actual martinis. Popular wisdom, however, dictates that if you toss the word "martini" into the title of a drink and pour something into a cocktail glass, you can convince the nouveau jet-set to shell out a couple of extra bucks for a very expensive beverage in a "martini bar." Regardless of their suspect relationship with the actual martini family, many of the beverages described below are delicious.

DRINKS CONTINUED IN THREE PAGES▶

FOR JUST A BRIEF MOMENT, TAKE A BREAK FROM THE HUSTLE
AND BUSTLE OF OUR WORKADAY WORLD AND JOIN US WHERE
THE GRITTY REALITY OF INTERSTATE TRUCK DRIVING MEETS
THE CULTIVATED INSOUCIANCE OF THE TRUST-FUND
GLITTERATI. WHERE THE BIGWIGS MEET THE BIG RIGS, AT A
LITTLE PLACE CALLED...

MARTINI TRUCK STOP
A ROMANCE OF THE ROAD

4:30 AM. Somewhere between Nowhere and Eastern Nowere along a
forgotten stretch of highway that wound through the thick, steamy veg-
etation of this Southern Gothic roadcape, I tried to sleepily focus my
high beams on the twisting double line ahead. Somewhere in the forest an owl shrieked. Somewhere, on a living room's raw wooden floor-
boards, a child is born.

Then, as my meandering beams sqirmed across the rough and
crumbling pavement of this ancient route, they glanced upon a small
wooden signpost, nearly swallowed up by the creeping kudzu, and
dying a slow rotting death at the hands of summer's swampy humidity.
Through the snarling vines I could pick out only a few
words...GAS...FOOD...DRINKS. A quick peek to my dashboard's gauges
confirmed my sleepy suspicions, if I didn't stop for gas soon, I'd have
to be stopping out here more permenantly. So, when I took this nearly
unmarked turn off the main road into the wet, green unknown, it seemed
to be my only hope. Who knew it would also turn out to be my only
salvation?

But after a few minutes in this cramped and twisting darkness, I
didn't know just what I was getting myself into. To be stranded on the
side of a somewhat major highway is one thing, to be stranded in the
middle of this ancient forest was quite another. Suddenly, without
warning, the road twisted around a tight corner and opened into the
biggest parking lot I had ever seen. At least three football fields from
tip to tail, this sea of macadam was nearly completely filled with dozens and dozens of 18-wheelers in all colors and sizes—featuring all

variety of advertised products on the side: the bigger ones had the more famous brands, like Jericho Automotive Parts and Elec-tro-Spun Sports Clothing, and smaller ones included the obscure and often entertaining local brands—Poppy's Paints, Big Green Bagelry, Tip Top Timber Goods, and the perplexing Flibbertyjibbers!. But where was the promised gas station? I couldn't see anything with all these trucks parked everywhere, and it really came as a shock to all-of-a-sudden come face to face with a small, unmarked building nestled unobtrusively between a Russell's Cold Transport cab and a MobileKing Custom Storage trailer. With a second look I noticed one small parking space, next to the door, exactly right for my little car. So I did what I guess I was fated to do: I parked, got out, and knocked on the front door.

A pause. Then...

A comically short gentleman in a beatifully tailored white tuxedo threw the door open, doffed an enormous top hat, looked straight up into my eyes, and smiled a toothy grin: "Welcome to Martini Truck Stop," he said, "We've been saving a seat for you."

As my eyes adjusted to the light of the inside, I could pick out the amazing, swirling detail of the place. Drivers of all shapes and sizes poured through the warren of small tables, flitting from one conversation to another, casually grabbing drinks off large round trays that the little waiters would almost magically appear with before disappearing just as quickly into the deep shadows of the corners. There were truckers in T-shirts and truckers in imported suits. There were ladies in sequinned gowns that dripped off their bodies like an early morning shower. Men and women moved together, joined at the crook of an arm, danced and spun for a moment, then broke apart to repeat the same ritual with another black suit, another white glove, another red dress. And the din of their chatter filled the hall with half-heard phrases and bubbling giggles, floating and popping the air, noticeably but inaudibly over the head of the assorted guests. Over the piano player stooped before his baby grand, cigarette dangling from one corner of his mouth, a half-full cocktail perched precariously by the keys.

"Sir, would you please follow me."

I looked down at my diminutive host. How long had I been staring out at this surprising scene? I could scarecely have been for more than just a few moments, since my eyes were still not completely adjusted, but I was still a little bit stunned and embarassed, and wasn't able to do anything but stammer, "Oh, oh yes. Yes."

With that, I watched the big white top hat dip into the crowd, and cut like a dorsal fin across to the far side side of the bar. I stood dazed for half a second, and then quickly followed.

STORY CONTINUED ON PAGE 82▶

DRY WIT

By now, you've probably noticed that the way to dry out a martini is to reduce the amount of vermouth in the drink. The extra-extra-dry martini is a frequently ordered drink—it sounds a lot more reputable than saying, "Hit me like a punching bag with three cold ounces of gin."

3 oz. gin

DRY MARTINI

1 part dry vermouth

10 parts gin

Pour a quick dash of vermouth into the shaker (half the shaker's rim) and then add a six-count (3 oz.) of gin. With such a high gin to vermouth ratio, it is impossible to eyeball proportions as recommended for other stirred cocktails. Garnish with two olives (pitted and without pimentos).

EXTRA-DRY MARTINI

1 splash vermouth

Splash the vermouth in the bottom of the shaker, swirl it around, then empty the shaker. Fill with ice, then pour 3 oz. gin. Stir and strain into martini glass, either straight up or on the rocks (ask the drinker which variant she prefers).

EXTRA-EXTRA-DRY MARTINI

3 oz. gin

Pour a six count of gin into a shaker filled with ice, strain into a cocktail glass, and make sure that the vermouth bottle doesn't even share a zip code with the gin. Garnish with two olives.

FIFTY-FIFTY

1½ oz. gin

1½ oz. dry vermouth

Stir in a shaker, strain into a cocktail glass, and garnish with two olives.

GIBSON

½ oz. dry vermouth

2½ oz. gin

Stir, strain contents into a cocktail glass, and garnish with cocktail onions.

VODKA MARTINI

½ oz. dry vermouth

2½ oz. vodka

Substitute vodka for the gin in a martini.

TEQUINI OR TEQUILA MARTINI
½ oz. dry vermouth

2½ oz. tequila

Substitute tequila for the gin in a martini.

BLACK MARTINI
1½ oz. vodka or gin

1½ oz. blackberry brandy or black raspberry liqueur

CHOCOLATE MARTINI
½ oz. crème de cacao

dash of orange liqueur (optional)

2 oz. vodka

COSMOPOLITAN
½ oz. triple sec

½ oz. lime juice

½ oz. cranberry juice

2 oz. vodka

Garnish with a lime.

FRENCH MARTINI
¾ oz. black raspberry liqueur

¾ oz. peach schnapps

1½ oz. vodka

Garnish with a cherry.

SAKETINI
½ oz. sake

2½ oz. gin

Garnish with lemon twist or olives.

MANHATTANS

Manhattans are very similar to martinis in terms of manufacture, but oh so different in their contents and flavor. Manhattans are generally made with dark alcohols and often use sweet (instead of dry) vermouth.

"PLEASE, DON'T BOTHER ME ON THIS PAGE."

MANHATTAN

½ oz. sweet vermouth
2½ oz. blended whiskey
Garnish with a cherry.

DRY MANHATTAN

½ oz. dry vermouth
2½ oz. blended whiskey

PERFECT MANHATTAN

1 part (¼ oz.) sweet vermouth
1 part (¼ oz.) dry vermouth
10 parts (2½ oz.) whiskey

You might want to measure these quantities using the rim of the shaker— rim half the shaker with dry vermouth, and the other half with sweet vermouth. Pour in a five count of whiskey, stir, strain, and garnish with a cherry.

RUM MANHATTAN

½ oz. sweet vermouth
2½ oz. rum

Substitute rum for the blended whiskey in a Manhattan. Garnish with a cherry.

TEQUILA MANHATTAN

½ oz. sweet vermouth
2½ oz. tequila

Substitute tequila for the blended whiskey in a Manhattan. Garnish with a cherry and a lime wedge.

ROB ROY

½ oz. sweet vermouth
2½ oz. Scotch

Substitute Scotch for the blended whiskey in a Manhattan. Garnish with a cherry.

COMFORT MANHATTAN

½ oz. sweet vermouth
2½ oz. Southern Comfort

Substitute Southern Comfort for the blended whiskey in a Manhattan. Garnish with a cherry.

LATIN MANHATTAN

1 oz. rum

1 oz. dry vermouth

1 oz. sweet vermouth

1 dash bitters

Garnish with a lemon twist.

GIMLETS

GIMLET

1 oz. Rose's lime juice

2 oz. gin

Stir and strain into a cocktail glass. Garnish with a lime wedge.

VODKA GIMLET

1 oz. Rose's lime juice

2 oz. vodka

Stir and strain into a cocktail glass. Garnish with a lime wedge.

STINGERS

STINGER

1½ oz. brandy

½ oz. crème de menthe

To make a sweet stinger, decrease the amount of brandy and increase the amount of delectable crème de menthe. If a drinker wants to have another form of alcohol substituted for brandy, she will generally specifically ask for a "Vodka Stinger" or a "Scotch Stinger."

☐ ☐ ☐ ☐ ☐ ☐ ☐ ☐ ☐

STINGERS
To remember that a stinger almost always contains crème de menthe, think of the stinging, cool flavor of the peppermint-flavored alcohol. Alternatively, keep in mind that the brandy bottle often stands next to the crème de menthe on the back bar so that the two may be quickly picked up.

For all practical purposes, the following drinks should be members of the stinger family.

PEPPERMINT PATTIE

1½ oz. dark crème de cacao

1½ oz. white crème de menthe

FLYING TIGER

1 oz. Galliano

1 oz. vodka

1 oz. white crème de menthe

This is a Galliano stinger with vodka.

OLD FASHIONEDS AND JULEPS

Old Fashioneds are prepared differently from other stirred cocktails. The following recipe is for the classic Old Fashioned, prepared with whiskey:

1. Put ½ tsp. of fine-grained sugar in the bottom of an Old Fashioned or other lowball glass. That little bump on the bottom of the Old Fashioned glass is there to remind you to do this.
2. Add a dash or two of bitters to the sugar.
3. Put a handful of ice cubes in the glass.
4. Pour in 2½ oz. of whiskey.
5. Add a splash of water or soda water.
6. Stir well. If you use soda water, then switch steps 5 and 6.
7. Garnish with a cherry, an orange slice, and a lemon twist.

□ □ □ □ □ □ □ □ □

JULEPS

In regions of the southern U.S., the mint julep is as much a religion as it is a drink. Attachment to certain recipes can approximate a form of fanaticism, and a misstep in producing a tasty julep is considered a form of sacrilege (such a mistake can get you killed in Lexington during the weekend of the Kentucky Derby). Consider the childhood (yes, childhood—there are now laws to prevent a return of these halcyon days) recollections of William Alexander Percy in his autobiographical Lanterns on the Levee, in which he vividly depicts his mother's recipe:

"Certainly her juleps had nothing in common with those hybrid concoctions one buys in bars the world over under that name. It would have been sacrilege to add lemon, or a slice of orange or of pineapple, or one of those wretched maraschino cherries. First you needed excellent bourbon whiskey; rye or Scotch would not do at all...You filled the glass, which apparently had no room left for anything else, with bourbon, the older the better, and grated a bit of nutmeg on the top. The glass immediately frosted and you settled back in your chair for half an hour of sedate cumulative bliss. Although you stirred the sugar at the bottom, it never all melted, therefore at the end of the half hour there was left a delicious mess of ice and mint and whiskey which a small boy was allowed to consume with calm rapture."

▶ "PLEASE, I MEAN IT. THIS IS MY PRIVATE TIME."

TEQUILA OLD FASHIONED
½ tsp. fine-grained sugar
1-2 dashes bitters
2½ oz. tequila

splash of water or soda water

RUM OLD FASHIONED
½ tsp. fine-grained sugar
1-2 dashes bitters
2½ oz. rum

splash of water or soda water

MINT JULEP
4 sprigs mint
1 tsp. powdered sugar
2 tsps. water
2½ oz. bourbon

In a silver julep cup, silver mug, or collins glass, grind the mint leaves, sugar, and water together (this can be accomplished by mashing the back of the spoon around the concoction). Fill the glass or mug with crushed ice, then add the bourbon. Top with more ice and garnish with a mint sprig.

BRANDY JULEP
4 sprigs mint
1 tsp. powdered sugar
2 tsps. water
2½ oz. brandy

Just substitute brandy for bourbon in a Mint Julep.

POPULAR STIRRED COCKTAILS

Although they aren't classics, you'll get many requests for these drinks in a professional bar, so you should memorize them. Now for the good news—drinkers usually prefer these on the rocks, so you can mix them right in the glass (a rocks glass) rather than wasting time transferring them from a shaker glass. The recipes are arranged according to common ingredients and variations, to help you memorize.

BLACK RUSSIAN
1½ oz. vodka
¾ oz. Kahlúa

DRINK CONTINUED ON NEXT PAGE▶

MUDSLIDE

1 oz. Kahlúa
1 oz. Irish cream
1 oz. vodka

This is very similar to a Black Russian, but it needs to be stirred diligently, since cream tends to resist mixing.

BRAVE BULL

1½ oz. tequila
1½ oz. Kahlúa

KAHLÚA AND AMARETTO

2 oz. Kahlúa
2 oz. amaretto

BLACK WATCH

1½ oz. Kahlúa
1½ oz. Scotch
splash of soda
Garnish with a lemon twist.

THE GODFATHER

½ oz. amaretto
1½ oz. Scotch

THE GODMOTHER

½ oz. amaretto
1½ oz. vodka

KAMIKAZE

1 oz. vodka
1 oz. triple sec
1 oz. lime juice

Mix with ice in a metal shaker, then strain into a cocktail or lowball glass.

RUSTY NAIL

½ oz. Drambuie
1½ oz. Scotch

B AND B

1 oz. brandy
1 oz. Benedictine
Stir gently.

GIN COCKTAIL

2 oz. gin

2 dashes bitters

Garnish with a lemon twist.

GIN AND IT

2 oz. gin

1 oz. sweet vermouth

Served neat (no ice used in the shaker or cocktail glass).

FUN STIRRED COCKTAILS

You won't get many requests for these drinks, but they're here in case you need them. Recipes are arranged alphabetically in this section. Most drinks should be prepared with crushed ice in a shaker and then poured into a cocktail glass.

BLANCHE

½ oz. curaçao

1 oz. anisette

1 oz. triple sec

BEAL'S COCKTAIL

½ oz. dry vermouth

½ oz. sweet vermouth

1½ oz. Scotch

BOMBAY COCKTAIL

¼ tsp. anisette

½ oz. triple sec

½ oz. dry vermouth

½ oz. sweet vermouth

1 oz. brandy

DUBONNET COCKTAIL

1½ oz. Dubonnet

1½ oz. gin

Garnish with a lemon twist.

EL PRESIDENTE

¾ oz. dry vermouth

1½ oz. light rum

□ □ □ □ □ □ □ □ □
FREESTYLING

One of the first important things to learn about bartending is that the wacky hijinks of Tom Cruise in the movie Cocktail require a spectator to suspend disbelief. As has been noted in other annals, movies don't always depict reality. And the reality of bartending, while glamorous, has no relationship to its wild, debauched portrayal in this flick. In point of fact, anyone who struts behind a bar and starts throwing around cocktail-shaking apparati will likely find himself drenched in cocktail ingredients and out of a job. Also, even if successfully pulled off, the time that it takes a bartender to throw all of those shakers around will lead to a drastic diminution of drinks made and, accordingly, tips received. For this reason, juggling bartenders, much like Santa Claus, are not real. And don't tell your children any differently!

DRINK CONTINUED ON THE NEXT PAGE▶

▶ "THAT DOES IT. I'M LEAVING. HAVE FUN READING THE REST OF THE BOOK"

1 dash bitters

Stir ingredients with ice and strain into a cocktail glass.

FLYING GRASSHOPPER
¾ oz. crème de menthe
¾ oz. white crème de cacao
1 oz. vodka

Stir with ice and strain into a cordial glass.

FRENCH BREEZE
1 oz. peppermint schnapps
2 oz. Pernod

GOLDEN GLOW
1 oz. Galliano
1 oz. Drambuie
1 oz. gin

The word "golden" should tip you off as to the presence of Galliano.

JELLY BEAN
1 oz. anisette
1 oz. blackberry brandy

KAHLÚA AND BRANDY
1½ oz. Kahlúa
1½ oz. brandy

NEGRONI
1 oz. gin
1 oz. Campari
1 oz. vermouth (either sweet or dry)
Garnish with a lemon twist.

ST. PATRICK'S DAY
1 oz. crème de menthe
1 oz. Chartreuse
1 oz. Irish whiskey
1 dash bitters

SAZERAC
1 tsp. sugar
dash bitters
dash Pernod

DRINK CONTINUED ON THE NEXT PAGE▶

2 oz. bourbon
Garnish with a lemon twist.

WANDERING MINSTREL
¾ oz. vodka
¾ oz. Kahlúa
¾ oz. brandy
¾ oz. white crème de menthe

YALE COCKTAIL
½ oz. dry vermouth
1 tsp. blue curaçao
dash bitters
1½ oz. gin

Those who wish to indulge further in the boorish manner of a Yalie should try either a bulldog highball (p. 51) or a bulldog (p. 43).

SHAKEN COCKTAILS

This part of bartending is fun and very professional looking once you get the hang of it. When you're starting out, be wary of going overboard and spilling all over yourself and innocent bystanders. (As a precautionary measure, please read "Freestyling," on page 69.) Follow the following procedure for all the basic shaken drinks and for all other shaken drinks served straight up. Don't be intimidated by the number of steps; shaken drinks are the easiest drinks to make, as you just have to dump in a few ingredients, give 'em a good shake, and then pour 'em out.

1. Fill the shaker glass two-thirds full with ice.
2. Pour in the ingredients.
3. Put the stainless steel shell over the shaker glass (as shown in the diagram placed slightly below this paragraph) and press down on the top to make a seal between the two. The steel shell is going to contract when the ice makes it cold, so the seal will get even stronger. That's the magic of science!

STEP4: SHAKE SHAKE SHAKE THE GLASS!!!

STEP 3: PUT THE SHAKER OVER THE GLASS. CAREFUL!!

STEP 5: PULL THE GLASS OUT OF THE SHAKER!!!!

4. Hold the top and bottom of the shaker and shake it up and down. Eventually you can get fancy in your shaking, but always make sure the ingredients go up and down in the glass.

5. You now need to break the seal. A gentle tap either against the heel of your hand or a surface should do. If the seal makes a loud snap as it breaks, don't be alarmed! Your drink is just breaking the tastiness barrier.

6. Keeping the shaker glass and shell together, turn the whole thing over. Then take the glass out of the steel shell. By turning the shaker over so that the shell is on the bottom you avoid making a mess.

7. Strain the drink from the shell into some type of lowball glass (preferably one with a stem so the drink will stay colder longer). The strainer should fit comfortably over the mouth of the shaker to prevent ice from entering the cocktail glass. Pour slowly so that the alcohol doesn't spill all over you.

STEP 5: HOLD THE STRAINER LIKE THIS!!!!

8. Garnish the drink as necessary.

STEP 7a: THIS IS WHAT POURING LOOKS LIKE.

9. Clean the shaker: pour in some water, shake it around, dump it out, and then wipe the inside. Some shaken cocktails have milk or cream in them, in which case take special pains in cleaning the shaker—nobody likes a whiskey sour garnished with chunks of curdled milk.

The recipes in the first two sections are arranged in groups of similar drinks to facilitate their mastery. You may find these recipes easy to

▶ "PRETTY FUN HERE, ALL BY YOURSELF, HUH?"
"NO, NOT SO FUN, I WISH YOU'D COME BACK, SCOTCH-GUY."
"WHATEVER, BUDDY. DON'T EXPECT A TIP."

"BUDDY."

remember before forging ahead into the real world only to encounter a new problem—you've memorized ingredients and proportions, but you forgot whether to shake or stir. For shame! As a general rule, shake fruit juice, sour mix, sugar, egg, and cream drinks, or drinks that contain other difficult-to-mix ingredients. Some of the multi-liqueur drinks in the stirred section might actually mix better when shaken.

Many of these recipes call for sour mix, a concoction made with juice from one-half lemon and a teaspoon of sugar. This ratio may be adjusted to your personal preference (or to the pre-fabbed bottle of sour mix that you buy), but it is a good idea always to have a bottle of sour mix on hand when tending bar; it will save you a lot of time when making shaken drinks.

BASIC SHAKEN COCKTAILS

SOURS

WHISKEY SOUR

2 oz. whiskey

1 oz. sour mix

Garnish with a cherry and an orange slice.

This basic recipe for sours is often varied slightly to create a number of similar beverages: amaretto sours, rum sours, tequila sours, and vodka sours.

WARD EIGHT

2 oz. whiskey

1 oz. sour mix

½ oz. grenadine

Garnish with a cherry and an orange slice.

SOUR BALL

1 oz. vodka

1 oz. apricot brandy

½ oz. sour mix

½ oz. orange juice

Garnish with orange and cherry.

DAIQUIRIS AND VARIATIONS

MAI TAIS

Vic Bergeron, known to friends and pirates as Trader Vic, is credited with the invention of the Mai Tai in 1944. He claims to have created the multifarious drink by mixing a 17-year-old rum with hints of orange curaçao flavoring, a touch of orgeat to create an almond residue, some lime, and rock candy syrup (rarely carried in the modern bar). While a wayfaring nomad named Don the Beachcomber claims that he patented the beverage, one is hard pressed to dispute the insistence of the late Trader Vic. Quoth Vic (shortly before his death): "I originated the Mai Tai. Many others have claimed credit. All this aggravates my ulcer completely. Anyone who says I didn't create this drink is a dirty stinker."

DAIQUIRI

2 oz. rum
juice of ½ lime
1 tsp. sugar

A daiquiri uses lime juice, not lemon, so avoid using sour mix in it. Some bars stock a pre-mixed lime and sugar mixture (such as Quik-Lime), but it is not very common. In a crowded, busy bar, some bartenders make daiquiris with sour mix (like a rum sour) and then squeeze a couple of lime wedges on top to fool the customer's taste buds.

BACARDI COCKTAIL

2 oz. Bacardi rum
1 oz. lime juice
1 tsp. grenadine

MAI TAI

2 oz. rum
½ oz. curaçao
½ oz. orgeat (almond syrup)
¾ oz. lime juice

Shake vigorously before adding a sprig of mint. Alternatively, garnish with pineapple and cherry. If you choose the latter path, you might as well stick an umbrella into the crowded drink to complete the tropical feel.

MARGARITAS

MARGARITA

2 oz. tequila
½ oz. triple sec
juice of ½ lime
Shake and strain into a salt-rimmed cocktail or champagne glass.

If you've forgotten how to create this salty effect, refer to "Salting Edges" on page 43.

COLLINSES

TOM COLLINS
2 oz. gin

1 oz. sour mix

Shake, strain into a collins glass, and top with a splash of soda water. Garnish with a cherry and an orange slice.

The main difference between sours and Collinses is the addition of soda water. Also, the sour is usually served without ice in a sour glass, whereas the Collins goes over ice into a highball like, frosted collins glass. The Vodka Collins, Rum Collins, and Tequila Collins are all fairly self-explanatory alterations to the original Tom Collins recipe. Just substitute the named alcohol for the gin in a Tom Collins.

JOHN COLLINS
2 oz. whiskey

1 oz. sour mix

Shake, strain into a collins glass, and top with a splash of soda water. Garnish with a cherry and an orange slice.

SLOE GIN FIZZ
2 oz. sloe gin

1 oz. sour mix

soda water to fill

SINGAPORE SLING
1½ oz. gin

¾ oz. wild cherry brandy

1 oz. sour mix

Shake, strain into a Collins glass, and top with soda water.

POPULAR SHAKEN COCKTAILS

Some of these drinks have become so popular in recent years that they're practically basics, so do memorize them if you plan to work in a bar some day. If you tend bar in a busy place, the whole shaker routine may become tiresome and begin to slow you down. To gain a little extra speed, use a half-shell shaker to short-shake drinks on the rocks. This gadget is a small, usually plastic shaker shell that fits over regular rocks and highball glasses. If you're using disposable plastic glasses, mix the drink in a highball glass and use a lowball glass for the half-shell.

Here are the steps for short-shaking:

1. Pour the drink ingredients over ice in the appropriate glass.
2. Fit the short-shaker securely over the glass.
3. Shake it up and down a few times.
4. Remove the shaker.

Quick and simple! This method is not as neat and thorough as the regular shaker technique, and cannot be used for straight-up cocktails, but it saves valuable time when you're in a hurry.

This section groups drinks with similar ingredients together in hopes of assisting in the process of their memorization.

GIN FIZZ

½ tsp. sugar

1½ oz. gin

1 oz. sour mix

dash of lime juice

Shake, then fill with soda water and garnish with a cherry.

ORANGE BLOSSOM

1½ oz. gin

1 oz. orange juice

¼ tbsp. powdered sugar

Shake with ice and strain into cocktail glass, then garnish with an orange.

GIN DAISY

2 oz. gin

1 oz. lemon juice or sour mix

1 tsp. grenadine

1 tsp. sugar

Shake with ice, strain into a highball glass, and fill with soda water. Garnish with an orange slice.

SOMBRERO

1½ oz. coffee brandy

milk or cream to fill

Serve over ice in a rocks glass. Some bartenders prefer not to shake their Sombreros, the idea being that the cream floats on top like a hat.

KAHLÚA SOMBRERO

1½ oz. Kahlúa

milk or cream to fill

WHITE RUSSIAN

2 oz. vodka

1 oz. Kahlúa or coffee brandy

½ oz. cream

Serve in a rocks glass. This drink, without the cream, is a Black Russian (a stirred drink).

DIRTY BIRD

An unstirred, unshaken White Russian.

IGUANA

½ oz. vodka

½ oz. tequila

½ oz. Kahlúa

1½ oz. sour mix (optional)

Shake all ingredients together, then strain into a cocktail glass. Garnish with a lime.

ITALIAN SOMBRERO

1½ oz. amaretto

milk or cream to fill

TOASTED ALMOND

1½ oz. Kahlúa or coffee brandy

1½ oz. amaretto

milk or cream to fill

Serve over ice in a rocks or highball glass.

ROASTED TOASTED ALMOND

1½ oz. vodka

1½ oz. Kahlúa or coffee brandy

1½ oz. amaretto

milk or cream to fill

ORGASM

¾ oz. amaretto

¾ oz. Kahlúa

¾ oz. Bailey's Irish cream

Shake over ice and strain into a cocktail glass.

NUTS AND BERRIES

1½ oz. Frangelico

1½ oz. Chambord

milk or cream to fill

Shake and strain into a highball glass.

GIRL SCOUT COOKIE

1 oz. vodka

1 oz. coffee liqueur

1 oz. peppermint schnapps

1 oz. cream or milk

CREAMSICLE

1½ oz. amaretto

1½ oz. orange juice

milk or cream to fill

Usually served over ice in a rocks or highball glass. This drink tastes like the ice cream bar of the same name.

RAZ-MA-TAZZ

1½ oz. Kahlúa

1½ oz. Chambord

milk or cream to fill

GRASSHOPPER

1 oz. green crème de menthe

1 oz. white crème de cacao

1 oz. cream

Serve in a rocks or cocktail glass (usually cocktail).

DIRTY GRASSHOPPER

1 oz. green crème de menthe

1 oz. Kahlúa

1 oz. milk

Serve in a rocks or cocktail glass (usually cocktail).

VODKA GRASSHOPPER
¾ oz. green crème de menthe
¾ oz. white crème de cacao
¾ oz. vodka
¾ oz. cream

Serve in a rocks or cocktail glass.

FLYING DUTCHMAN
2 oz. gin
1 dash triple sec

Shake with ice and strain into and old-fashioned glass over ice.

ALEXANDER
1 oz. gin
1 oz. dark crème de cacao
1 oz. cream or milk

Serve in a rocks or cocktail glass

ALEXANDER'S SISTER
1 oz. gin
1 oz. green crème de menthe
1 oz. cream or milk

This is also sometimes referred to as a Susanna.

BRANDY ALEXANDER
1 oz. brandy
1 oz. dark crème de cacao
1 oz. cream or milk

Dust the top with nutmeg.

PINK SQUIRREL
1 oz. crème de noyaux
1 oz. crème de cacao
1 oz. cream

Usually served straight up in a cocktail glass. Memorize these ingredients by remembering that crème de noyaux is red and when mixed with cream it becomes pink. Squirrels eat nuts; crème de noyaux is almond flavored.

DRINKS CONTINUED IN THREE PAGES▶

STORY CONTINUED FROM PAGE 59▶

MARTINI TRUCK STOP PART 2

I followed the bobbing top hat through a lavishly decorated archway, which I couldn't be sure was asian or north african. A beaded curtain opened up, and the pungent aroma of honey tobacco rose out, carried on slippery blue-gray tendrils that pooled on the ceiling, then thinned and vanished.

"Your seat is just a little bit further. Please, come this way."

This new room was thick with smoke, and it wasn't until I was a few feet away did I notice my eventual destination. Like the ghost of the *Marie Celeste* rising out of the ocean fog, a plush multicolored island of pillows and drapery rushed forward to meet me. At its summit, a huge mountain of a man, with forearms the size of ham hocks, and in his fleshy fist, a martini of such ghastly proportion one might suspect it could never be finished. The man flicked his wrist, and with one casual gulp swallowed the lot of it—lemon twist and all. He turned, handed the glass off to an attendant waiter who silently rushed off. From the back of his plush throne, the man produced a cudgel of a cigar, lit it slowly, filled his mouth with a drag, and began to speak.

"Please, have a seat, we have been expecting you."

Smoke billowed from his mouth as he spoke, obscuring his face, and rushing over the top of his bald head. I looked to the side, and noticed that my guide was no longer there. This was not particularly surprising. What *was* surprising was that a large chair had appeared in his place, upholstered in deep red velvet, with armrests carved into the form of vigilant cherubs. I ran my fingers over their tiny faces and sat down. The large man had just taken another drag off his cigar, signalling his desire to speak again.

"So, what do you think about Martini Truck Stop?" he said, or, rather, *poured*, since thick rivulets of smoke dripped from his fleshy lips with every syllable.

I had nothing really to say.

Another drag.

"You must be impressed. Pretty much everyone is," he continued, as if paying my silence no mind, "People seem to like the atmosphere...they find it to be a nice change of pace from the other greasy spoons on the main trucking line from New York to Atlanta..."

As he spoke, I looked around the room. Seeing the bend of an arm, the orange glow of a cigarette butt, and the sheer whisper of silk dresses materialize and dissolve into the atmosphere.

"You can call me Mister El," said the man, breaking into my little dream, "In fact, I insist. Please, do speak up, you must have something to say."

"Mister El, I don't know what to say. Um, my name is..."

"We know," interrupted Mister El, "We *know*."

"Well, I think I'd like a drink."

Before I had finished my sentence, there was one of those big round trays at my side, on it, a Manhattan, a Maker's Mark Manhattan. My favorite. Of course. The glass was almost frosty to the touch, as though it had been kept in the freezer until just before the drink was poured. I took a sip.

"It's perfect isn't it?" said Mister El.

"Of course."

Mister El settled into his pile and spread his toes over the green satin of an overstuffed pillow.

"If you're wondering why you're here and why we've been expecting you, I can't tell you. I don't even know myself." Under my fingers I felt the carved angels' eyes, their noses, their waves of hair. "I *do* know that Martini Truck Stop can do strange things to a man, and when it calls its siren call, there are few powerful enough to resist it, or even to know they are being called. I came here over 20 years ago, in the middle of hauling a load of television parts to a distributor in Maryland. The truck is still sitting out in some far corner of the lot. The keys are still hanging on the rack in the foyer."

As he spoke, I found I was having trouble focusing on small objects.

"If I'm right, I don't think you'll ever want to see your sister and your family in Tucson again."

"Wait," I said, suddenly able to focus on small objects, "What was that?"

"I *said*," repeated Mister El, "If I'm right, I don't think you'll ever want to see your sister and your family in Tucson again."

I'm an only child. I'm adopted. I'm from Vermont.

"I really think I should be going."

"Wait, if I'm right, you'll never want to leave"

I am walking out the door.

"Your name is Peter Vandermarck."

That's a lie.

"You are not driving home right now!"

I am driving home right now.

BANSHEE

1 oz. crème de banane
1 oz. white crème de cacao
1 oz. cream

Usually served straight up in a cocktail glass. This drink is similar to a Pink Squirrel, but with crème de banane instead of crème de noyaux. (Banshee and banana are also alliterative.)

MELONBALL

1½ oz. Midori
¾ oz. vodka
orange juice to fill

Serve over ice in a highball glass. Garnish with orange.

PEARL HARBOR

2 oz. Midori
1 oz. vodka
pineapple juice to fill

Serve over ice in a highball glass. Garnish with cherry and pineapple.

ALABAMA SLAMMER

¾ oz. Southern Comfort
¾ oz. vodka
¾ oz. amaretto
dash grenadine
splash orange juice

Serve in a highball, cocktail, or shot glass. For a slightly stronger drink, substitute sloe gin for grenadine. Be sure to ask if the drinker wants a highball or a shot and then vary the amounts of the ingredients accordingly, maintaining an equal ratio between the Southern Comfort and the vodka.

APRICOT BOMB

1½ oz. apricot brandy
2 oz. vodka
1½ oz. triple sec
2 oz. sour mix

Serve over ice in a highball glass.

CHERRY BOMB

1½ oz. cherry brandy
2 oz. vodka

1½ oz. triple sec
2 oz. sour mix

Serve over ice in a highball glass.

SCARLETT O'HARA

1½ oz. Southern Comfort
1½ oz. cranberry juice
dash of lime juice
Garnish with lime.

Think of Scarlett and remember that scarlet cranberry juice gives the drink its red color. Scarlett O'Hara of Gone With the Wind *reminds most people of the South, so it should be easy to remember the Southern Comfort.*

ZOMBIE

¾ oz. light rum
¾ oz. dark rum
1½ oz. Jamaican rum
2 oz. pineapple juice
1 oz. lime juice
1 oz. orange juice

Shake and strain into a highball glass over fresh ice. Float on top ½ oz. of 151-proof rum. Garnish with a pineapple slice or chunk and a cherry. Serve with straws.

ZOMBIE (VARIATION)

1 oz. light rum
½ oz. Jamaican rum
½ oz. crème de noyaux
½ oz. triple sec
1 oz. lemon juice
1 oz. orange juice

Shake, strain into a highball glass over fresh ice, and top with soda water. Garnish with a pineapple slice or chunk and a cherry. There are limitless numbers of variations on the zombie. The common denominator to all recipes, however, is that they include as many different kinds of rum as possible while obscuring the taste of the alcohol to the greatest possible degree, thereby turning a reveling drinker into a member of the walking dead.

ICED TEA

1 oz. vodka

DRINK CONTINUED ON THE NEST PAGE▶

1 oz. gin
1 oz. tequila
1 oz. triple sec
splash of lemon juice

Shake, strain into a highball glass over fresh ice, and fill with cola. See page 52 for a slightly different recipe.

COMFORTABLE PIRATE

1½ oz. Captain Morgan's spiced rum
1 oz. Southern Comfort
pineapple juice to fill

Shake and strain into a highball glass over fresh ice. Garnish with a member of the Village People.

□ □ □ □ □ □ □ □ □

PUNCH

At first glance, these Planter's Punch recipes would appear to be quite difficult to remember. As chance would have it, they are. Still, it's easy to cheat if you have a bottle of Myers's rum in front of you—you'll find a recipe printed up right on the label. Cheers!

PLANTER'S PUNCH

2 oz. rum
1 oz. Myers's rum (Jamaican)
1 tsp. sugar
juice of 1 lime
fill with equal parts orange and pineapple juice

Shake, strain into a highball glass over fresh ice, and fill with soda water. Garnish with an orange slice and a cherry.

PLANTER'S PUNCH (VARIATION)

2 oz. rum
1 oz. sour mix
splash orange juice
splash pineapple juice

Shake, strain into a highball glass over fresh ice, then swirl on top ½ oz. Myers's rum (Jamaican) and ½ oz. curaçao. Garnish with a cherry and an orange slice. Serve with a straw. The liquors on top give the drink its "punch" when it is sipped through a straw. The drinker finishes the bottom part first and gets an extra boost from the rum and curaçao at the end.

EGGNOGS

STANDARD EGGNOG

1 egg
1 tsp. sugar

1½ oz. liquor (brandy, whiskey, rum, or a combination)

4 oz. milk

Shake with ice and strain into a highball glass without ice. Dust with nutmeg.

BREAKFAST EGGNOG

1 egg

½ oz. triple sec

2 oz. apricot brandy

4 oz. milk

Shake with ice and strain into a highball glass without ice. Dust with nutmeg.Goes great with Wheaties for that extra-special breakfast of champions. For an extra-foamy nog, try mixing these eggnogs in the blender.

FUN SHAKEN COCKTAILS

Just glance through these drinks to see if they sound good, but don't worry about memorizing them. They are listed alphabetically for easy reference.

BETWEEN THE SHEETS

1 oz. brandy

1 oz. triple sec

1 oz. rum

dash lemon juice or sour mix

Shake and strain into a cocktail glass.

BULLSHOT

1½ oz. vodka

4 oz. beef bouillon

dash Worcestershire sauce

dash salt and pepper (optional)

Shake with ice, strain into a highball glass with ice, and garnish with a lemon twist.

CALIFORNIA LEMONADE

2 oz. blended whiskey

1 oz. sour mix

juice of 1 lime

dash grenadine

Shake, strain into a collins glass over fresh ice, and fill with soda water. Garnish with an orange slice, a lemon twist, and a cherry.

CHERRY RUM

1½ oz. rum
½ oz. cherry brandy
½ oz. cream

Shake well and strain into a cocktail glass over ice.

CHOCOLATE MINT RUM

1 oz. rum
½ oz. dark crème de cacao
1 oz. white crème de menthe
½ oz. cream

Shake well and strain into a cocktail glass.

CHUCKIE

1½ oz. vodka
dash curaçao
splash pineapple juice
splash orange juice

Shake and strain into a rocks glass over fresh ice, and top with soda. Garnish with a cherry.

CREAM PUFF

2 oz. rum
1 oz. cream
1 tsp. sugar

Shake and strain into a highball glass over fresh ice.

CREAMY MOCHA MINT

¾ oz. Kahlúa or coffee brandy
¾ oz. white crème de cacao
¾ oz. white crème de menthe
¾ oz. cream

Shake and strain into a rocks glass over fresh ice.

CRIMSON COCKTAIL

1½ oz. gin
2 tsps. lemon juice
1 tsp. grenadine
¾ oz. port

Shake the gin, lemon juice, and grenadine, strain into a cocktail glass, and float port on top. Hold sway while drinking!

CUBAN SPECIAL

1 oz. rum
dash triple sec
splash pineapple juice
juice of ½ lime

Shake and strain into a rocks glass over fresh ice. Garnish with a cherry.

DIRTY MOTHER

1½ oz. Kahlúa or coffee brandy
1½ oz. brandy

Shake and strain into a rocks or highball glass over fresh ice. For a slight variation, one can add 1 oz. of cream. Some people refer to this as a dirty white mother.

EL PRESIDENTE HERMINIO

1½ oz. rum
½ oz. crème de banane
½ oz. curaçao
splash orange juice
splash pineapple juice

Shake and strain into a lowball glass over fresh ice.

FAN

2 oz. Scotch
1 oz. triple sec or Cointreau
1 oz. grapefruit juice

Shake and strain into a rocks glass over fresh ice.

GEORGIA CREAM

1 oz. peach brandy
1 oz. white crème de cacao
1 oz. cream

Shake and strain into a rocks glass over fresh ice.

GOLDEN APPLE

1 oz. Galliano
½ oz. applejack
½ oz. white crème de cacao

Shake and strain into a champagne glass rimmed with maraschino cherry juice and dipped in coconut powder.

GOLDEN DREAM

1 oz. Galliano
½ oz. triple sec or Cointreau
½ oz. cream
½ oz. orange juice

Shake and strain into a cocktail glass or a rocks glass over fresh ice.

GUANA GRABBER

1 oz. light rum
1 oz. dark rum
1 oz. coconut rum (such as Malibu or Cocoribe)
3 oz. pineapple juice
1 oz. grapefruit juice
dash grenadine

Shake and strain into a rocks glass over fresh ice.

HARVARD

1½ oz. five-star brandy
½ oz. sweet vermouth
1 dash bitters
1 tsp. grenadine
juice of ½ lemon

Shake and strain into a cocktail glass. Garnish with a lemon twist. A fair drink, to be sure, but as fair as Harvard?

HAWAIIAN

2 oz. gin
1 tbsp. pineapple juice
½ oz. triple sec

Shake with ice and strain into a cocktail glass.

HOT PANTS

1½ oz. tequila
½ oz. peppermint schnapps
1 tbsp. grapefruit juice
1 tsp. powdered sugar

Shake with ice and pour into a rocks glass rimmed with salt. For a reminder on how to salt a glass, see "Salting Edges" on page 43. Drink while wearing short shorts.

JACK ROSE

2 oz. applejack

juice of ½ lemon
1 tsp. grenadine

Shake and strain into a rocks glass over fresh ice. Garnish with a lemon.

JAMAICAN CREAM

1 oz. Jamaican rum
1 oz. triple sec
1 oz. cream

Shake and strain into a rocks glass over fresh ice.

JAMES BOND

"A vodka martini, shaken, not stirred." (However, Bond once ordered bourbon, no ice.)

MEXICANA

1½ oz. tequila
1 oz. lemon juice
dash grenadine
1 tbsp. pineapple juice

Shake with ice and strain into a cocktail glass.

MOCHA CREAM

1 oz. Kahlúa or coffee brandy
1 oz. white crème de cacao
1 oz. cream

Shake and strain into a rocks glass over fresh ice.

MOCHA MINT

¾ oz. coffee liqueur or coffee brandy
¾ oz. white crème de menthe
¾ oz. white crème de cacao

Shake all ingredients with ice, strain into a cocktail glass, and serve.

PINK LADY

2 oz. gin
1 oz. cream
½ oz. grenadine
1 egg white

Shake and strain into a cocktail glass.

POPPY COCKTAIL

1½ oz. gin
¾ oz. white crème de cacao

Shake and strain into a cocktail glass.

RAMOS FIZZ

1½ oz. gin
juice of ½ lemon
juice of ½ lime
1½ oz. cream
½ tsp. sugar
1 egg white
1 tsp. orange juice

Shake and strain into a rocks glass over fresh ice. Top with club soda.

RED RUSSIAN

1 oz. strawberry liqueur
1 oz. vodka
1 oz. cream

Shake and strain into a rocks glass over fresh ice.

RUSSIAN BEAR

1 oz. vodka
1 oz. dark crème de cacao
1 oz. cream

Shake and strain into a rocks glass over fresh ice.

SIDECAR

1 oz. brandy
½ oz. triple sec
juice of ½ lemon

Shake and strain into a cocktail glass.

SPANISH MOSS

1½ oz. tequila
1 oz. Kahlúa

Shake, strain into a cocktail glass, and add three drops of green crème de menthe.

TAM-O'-SHANTER (IRISH SOMBRERO)
1 oz. Kahlúa or coffee brandy
1 oz. Irish whiskey
milk to fill

Shake with ice in a highball glass.

TEQUILA MOCKINGBIRD
1½ oz. tequila
¾ oz. green crème de menthe
juice of 1 lime

Shake with ice and strain into cocktail glass. Garnish with a lime slice.

TOOTSIE ROLL
1½ oz. Kahlúa
1½ oz. dark crème de cacao
orange juice to fill

Shake with ice in a highball glass. When made correctly, this drink tastes like the eponymous candy.

TROPICAL GOLD
1½ oz. rum
½ oz. crème de banane
orange juice to fill

Shake with ice in a highball glass. Garnish with an orange slice and a

PINEAPPLE CHUNK.
velvet kiss
1 oz. gin
½ oz. crème de banane
1 oz. cream
splash pineapple juice
splash grenadine

Shake with ice in a highball glass.

FROZEN DRINKS

Frozen drinks (also called freezes or blended drinks) taste incredibly delicious. Even the most stubborn and steadfast beer or whiskey drinkers have trouble refusing a frosty piña colada on a hot day.

BLENDED INSANITY

Most blenders range from 24 to 48 oz. in capacity. Since a typical highball glass holds about 12 oz., adjust the ingredient amounts to fit your blender while making sure that you maintain the proportions of the original recipe. In most recipes, the blender will be approximately three-quarters full. As with the ingredients, the exact amount of ice will vary, but simply eyeballing the right amount should be sufficient. In general, increasing the amount of ice in the blender will result in a thicker drink.

To make blender drinks, follow these few simple steps:

1. Use only a heavy-duty blender. Those wheezing household blenders lack the teeth and the courage to successfully cut the ice. Wrap the blender in cellophane to avoid creating a horrible mess.

2. With the motor off, mix the ingredients in the blender. You can either put the liquor into the blender or leave it out. Given the vast number of people who enjoy the virgin alternatives to frozen drinks, however, we recommend pouring the alcohol directly into the serving glass instead of the blender. That way, you don't have to wash the blender before preparing a virgin version of these drinks. Fill the blender about a quarter of the way with ice, then add the mixers until the ice just starts to float.

3. Put the lid on.

4. Keeping fingers, hair, loose clothing, and small children at a safe distance, hold the lid down with one hand and start the machine on low speed. After the initial mixing, change to high speed until the ingredients are well blended.

5. Pour the mixture over alcohol in the glass. Stir with a straw or spoon to circulate the alcohol throughout the concoction.

The following recipes are divided into five categories to help you memorize the ones you like: Coladas, Daiquiris, Margaritas, Tropical Drinks, and Ice Cream Drinks.

COLADAS

PIÑA COLADA

2 oz. rum

1 oz. coconut cream (comes in a can at the supermarket or liquor store)

2 oz. pineapple juice

Blend with ice. Garnish with a cherry and a pineapple chunk. If you don't want to measure or use the amounts given in this recipe (in other words, if you just want to throw the ingredients in the blender any old way), follow this basic formula:

as much rum as you want (2 parts)
1 part coconut cream
2 parts pineapple juice

PACK THE PIÑA PUNCH

If you don't want a sweet piña colada, reduce the amount of coconut cream.

For a slushy drink, add more ice.

For a special touch, add a splash of grenadine and you'll have pink piñas.

For a richer rum flavor, use golden or dark rum as well as light rum.

MIDORI COLADA

2 oz. Midori
1 oz. rum
4 oz. pineapple juice
2 oz. coconut cream

Blend with ice. Garnish with a cherry, pineapple chunk, or melonball.

DAIQUIRIS

FROZEN DAIQUIRI

2 oz. rum
½ oz. triple sec
1½ oz. lime juice
1 tsp. sugar

Blend with ice.

BANANA DAIQUIRI

2 oz. rum
½ oz. crème de banane (optional)
1 sliced banana
1½ oz. lime juice

Blend with ice.

☐☐☐☐☐☐☐☐☐
DAIQUIRIS
You can keep adjusting the frozen daiquiri recipe for any fruit in the world. If you have a favorite fruit or flavoring, throw it into the blender with some rum, sour mix, and ice. As an optional inclusion, toss in an appropriately flavored liqueur for that special sauce (for instance, include Chambord in a raspberry daiquiri).

PEACH DAIQUIRI

2 oz. rum

½ oz. peach schnapps or peach-flavored brandy

½ cup fresh or canned peaches

dash of lime juice

Blend with ice.

STRAWBERRY DAIQUIRI

2 oz. rum

½ oz. strawberry liqueur

½ cup fresh or frozen strawberries

1 oz. lime juice

1 tsp. sugar

Blend with ice.

MARGARITAS

MARGARITA

1½ oz. tequila

½ oz. triple sec

1 oz. lime juice

Blend with or without ice. Garnish with a lime slice (optional), and serve in a cocktail or champagne glass rimmed with salt. Always salt the rim before mixing yer margarita. If you've forgotten how to salt the rim of a glass, refer to "Salting Edges" on page 43.

STRAWBERRY MARGARITA

2 oz. tequila

1 oz. triple sec

4 oz. lemon or lime juice

½ cup strawberries, fresh or frozen

1 oz. strawberry liqueur or 2 tsp. sugar

Blend with ice. Garnish with a fresh strawberry or a lime slice. Serve in a cocktail or champagne glass.

MIDORI MARGARITA

2 oz. tequila

1½ oz. Midori

1½ oz. sour mix

Blend with ice. Serve in a salted cocktail or champagne glass (salt optional).

TROPICAL DRINKS

SCORPION

2 oz. light rum

½ oz. brandy

2 oz. lemon juice

2 oz. orange juice

Blend with ice. Garnish with a cherry and an orange slice.

BLUE HAWAIIAN

1 oz. light rum

1 oz. blue curaçao

1 oz. cream of coconut

2 oz. pineapple juice

Blend with ice. Garnish with pineapple. Consume while wearing Blue Suede Shoes.

JUMP UP AND KISS ME

½ oz. Galliano

1½ oz. rum

½ oz. apricot brandy

juice of 1 lemon

1 oz. pineapple juice

½ egg white

Blend with ice. Serve in a brandy snifter.

GOLDEN CADILLAC (NOT REALLY TROPICAL, BUT EH!)

1 oz. Galliano

1 oz. white crème de cacao

1 oz. cream

Combine with a third-cup of crushed ice in a blender at low speed for 10 seconds. Pour into a chilled cocktail or champagne glass.

ICE CREAM DRINKS

MISSISSIPPI MUD

1½ oz. Southern Comfort
1½ oz. Kahlúa or coffee brandy
2 scoops vanilla ice cream

Blend without ice. Garnish with chocolate shavings.

HUMMER

1 oz. Kahlúa or coffee brandy
1 oz. light rum
2 scoops vanilla ice cream

Blend without ice.

BLENDED WHITE RUSSIAN

1 oz. Kahlúa
2 oz. vodka
2 scoops vanilla ice cream

Blend without ice. Sprinkle with chocolate shavings.

SHOTS

It's inevitable—in any bar on a given night, there's going to be a group of folks appearing with a commitment to reliving the splendor of Animal House. These people aren't evil, per se, although their titanic appetites for fun can often get the best of them. Before entering into a career of dishing out shots to the irrepressible, it's definitely a good idea to look over Chapter 8 on alcohol safety.

The mechanics of producing shots can range in difficulty from fantastically simple to profoundly baffling. Keep in mind that most people expect their shots chilled (to make them go down more easily). To do this, just fill a metal shaker about a quarter of the way with ice before pouring in the alcohol, then strain the liquor into the shot glasses. The amount of liquor that you want to pour into a shot glass varies between different establishments, generally ranging between 2 and 3 oz.

Since shots are generally consumed in groups, a bartender can simplify her job by mastering the art of preparing multiple shots. To do so, follow these simple steps:

1. Line up the glasses for the number of drinks you'll need. This is an especially good idea, since this will prevent you from forgetting how many drinks you're supposed to prepare.

2. Fill a metal shaker half way with ice before pouring in the alcohol. When adding the alcohol, prepare enough booze for one extra drink if more than three drinks have been ordered at once. For reasons that defy explanation, the preparation of shots disproves the scientific logic that matter cannot be destroyed, and you'll often find yourself short of the necessary quantity (especially if you have problems with spillage—an inevitability when preparing lots of shots).

3. Strain equal amounts into each glass. You'll be happy that you prepared too much at this point, since you can pour the excess into the glasses to level them off. Generally, you should underpour the first couple of glasses so that you have some liquor with which to top off the needy glasses.

MIXED SHOTS

B-52

½ oz. Grand Marnier

½ oz. Bailey's Irish Cream

½ oz. Kahlúa

Serve straight up in a shot glass. Some fancy bartenders like to layer these alcohols in reverse order.

BLOW JOB

½ oz. Bailey's Irish Cream

½ oz. Kahlúa

small glob of whipped cream on top

This is served straight up in a shot glass. The drinker puts his or her mouth entirely over the shot glass and cranes the neck back to drink. No hands allowed! Not in the ever-classy Blow Job. Call your proud parents when you've finished this fine night out.

BRAIN

¾ oz. Kahlúa

¾ oz. peach schnapps

splash of Bailey's Irish Cream

Do not stir! Usually served straight up in a shot glass. It's the swirling of the Bailey's, which should be added last, that creates the "brain" texture.

BRAIN HEMORRHAGE

¾ oz. Kahlúa

¾ oz. peach schnapps

splash of Bailey's Irish Cream

splash of grenadine

Gently pour grenadine on top of a brain. This is your brain on booze.

BUFFALO SWEAT

1 oz. bourbon

several dashes Tabasco sauce

Wring the bar rag into the drink. Serve straight up in a shot glass.

This drink is a popular "rite-of-passage" drink especially suitable to 21st birthdays. Occasionally a customer will ask you to surprise them with something unusual—a Buffalo Sweat will usually do the trick, especially if you're in a vindictive mood. You may opt for something a little less "challenging" if the patron does not resemble a grizzly werewolf.

CEMENT MIXER

1 oz. Bailey's Irish Cream

1 oz. lime juice

The drinker leans his or her head back and the bartender pours a shot of each ingredient into the open mouth. The swirling effect of the ingredients (which results in a shockingly pleasant congealing process) coupled with its unusual method of consumption gives this drink its name.

DEAD NAZI

1 oz. Jägermeister

1 oz. peppermint schnapps

Serve straight up in a shot glass. The liquors should be cold.

FIREBALL

1 oz. cinnamon schnapps

dash Tabasco sauce

Serve straight up in a shot glass.

GRAPE CRUSH

¾ oz. vodka

¾ oz. Chambord

splash sour mix

Shake with ice and strain into a shot glass.

HURRICANE

¾ oz. Jägermeister

¾ oz. Yukon Jack

splash of Bailey's Irish Cream

Do not shake or stir this shot. The Bailey's will create a stormy effect that makes the Dark and Stormy look like a "Sunny Day/ Chasin' the clouds away./ On my way to where the air is sweet/Can you tell me how to get,/ How to get to Sesame Street."

JELL-O SHOTS

12 oz. vodka

12 oz. water

6 oz. Jell-O gelatin mix (any flavor)

Mix 6 oz. of vodka with 6 oz. of water and bring to a boil. Stir in Jell-O gelatin mix. Remove from stove and add remaining 6 oz. of water and 6 oz. of vodka. Let set in refrigerator overnight. The "shots" can be semigelatinous and drinkable or jelled and eaten with a spoon. Remove the mix from the refrigerator earlier if you do not want solidified Jell-O.

The drinker should be aware that because Jell-O shots are not completely liquid the alcohol takes slightly longer to be absorbed into the bloodstream, delaying its effect. For more information on the physiology of alcohol absorption, see Chapter 8.

LEMON DROP

¾ oz. Absolut Citron

¾ oz. triple sec

Serve straight up in a shot glass. Give the drinker a lemon slice dipped in sugar as a chaser.

ORANGE CRUSH

¾ oz. vodka

¾ oz. triple sec

orange juice to fill

Serve straight up in a shot glass.

PRAIRIE FIRE

1½ oz. tequila

tabasco sauce to fill

Serve straight up in a shot glass.

SNAKEBITE

1½ oz. Yukon Jack

juice of ½ lime

Serve straight up in a shot glass.

TEQUILA POPPER

1 oz. tequila

1 oz. ginger ale

Cover the shot glass with a napkin and hand, then slam it on the table top. Drink while foaming.

TERMINATOR

½ oz. Jägermeister

½ oz. Bailey's Irish Cream

½ oz. peppermint schnapps

½ oz. bourbon

Serve straight up in a shot glass. Drink enough of these and the contents of your stomach will be threatening, "I'll be back."

WINDEX

¾ oz. vodka

¾ oz. blue curaçao

Serve straight up in a shot glass.

WOO WOO

¾ oz. vodka

¾ oz. peach schnapps

cranberry juice to fill

Stir, then strain into a shot glass.

LAYERED SHOTS

With the exception of floating fruit in Jell-O, perhaps the greatest culinary mystery remains the elegant production of beautiful and distinct layers of alcohol in a shot glass. Layered shots, also known as pousse-cafés, are perhaps the most scientifically demanding of drinks, in addition to being the most time-consuming drinks to prepare. When you pour several liquids carefully into a shot glass, the heaviest ones stay on the bottom and the lightest ones float to the top, thus creating layers. To make these drinks, be careful, and for the love of God, have patience! If you pour too quickly, your alcohol won't float, and your masterpiece will be destroyed. The following steps provide the appropriate protocol for pouring layered shots:

1. Tip the bar spoon upside down and lower it into the glass until it is just resting atop the alcohol and touching the side of the glass.
2. Lower the speedpourer down as close to the back of the bar spoon as is humanly possible. Keep your index finger firmly nestled over the air hole on the back of the speedpourer to slow down the rate at which the liquor flows. Always pour the heaviest liquid first, then the next heaviest, and so on.
3. Since you're keeping your finger over the air hole, the three-count technique becomes useless. Instead, eyeball the liquid to a height of about a quarter inch. That will roughly approximate 1 oz.
4. Success! Oooh, pretty!

If your task merely consists of "floating" an ingredient, you will need far less precision. Just lower the speed pourer as close as possible to the top of the drink and give it about a splash (a one count). Floated alcohols are invariably less dense than their sunken counterparts and will stay atop their brethren.

The recipes here list the ingredients from heaviest to lightest, so pour them in the given order. Pour just enough of each liquid to get a smooth, flat layer, but feel free to experiment with the proportions listed here to change the thickness of the layers.

ANGEL'S DELIGHT
1 part grenadine
1 part triple sec
1 part Crème Yvette
1 part cream

ANGEL'S KISS

1 part white crème de cacao
1 part Crème Yvette
1 part brandy
1 part cream

ANGEL'S TIP

1 part dark crème de cacao
1 part cream

Stick a toothpick through a cherry and balance it on top of the glass.

ANGEL'S WING

1 part white crème de cacao
1 part five-star brandy
1 part cream

CHRISTMAS

1 part grenadine
2 parts green crème de menthe

FIFTH AVENUE

1 part dark crème de cacao
1 part apricot brandy
1 part cream

KING ALPHONSE

1 part brown crème de cacao
1 part cream

This is an Angel's Tip without the cherry.

KING'S CUP

2 parts Galliano
1 part cream

PRINCESS

3 parts apricot brandy
1 part cream

STARS AND STRIPES

1 part grenadine
1 part heavy cream
1 part blue curaçao

"HEY!"

"HEY!"

OH MY GOSH! LOOK AT THESE ANIMALS! WHAT ARE THEY DOING HERE!? OH MY GOSH! OH MY GOSH! WHO KNOWS!?!

"HEY!"

LIQUEUR	RELATIVE WEIGHT
Anisette (50 proof)	17.8
Crème de noyaux (50 proof)	17.7
Crème de menthe (60 proof)	15.9
Crème de banane (50 proof)	15.0
Maraschino liqueur (50 proof)	14.9
Coffee liqueur (50 proof)	14.2
Cherry liqueur (48 proof)	12.7
Parfait Amour (50 proof)	12.7
Blue curaçao (60 proof)	11.7
Blackberry liqueur (50 proof)	11.2
Apricot liqueur (58 proof)	10.0
Orange curaçao (60 proof)	9.8
Triple sec (60 proof)	9.8
Coffee brandy (70 proof)	9.0
Peach brandy (70 proof)	7.0
Cherry brandy (70 proof)	6.8
Blackberry brandy (70 proof)	6.7
Apricot brandy (70 proof)	6.6
Rock and Rye liqueur (60 proof)	6.5
Ginger brandy (70 proof)	6.1
Peppermint schnapps (60 proof)	5.2
Kümmel (78 proof)	4.2
Peach liqueur (60 proof)	4.1
Sloe gin (60 proof)	4.0

MAKE YOUR OWN LAYERED SHOTS

Each liqueur has a specific weight. The key to making pousse-cafés is to put the heaviest liqueur in the glass first, then the next heaviest, and so on. Cream floats on the top. Technically, you could probably layer all of the liqueurs listed here on top of each other, but most layered shots have only three to five layers. The chart to the left assigns numbers to the relative weights of the most popular layered-shot ingredients, from heaviest to lightest. Bon chance!

OH MY GOSH!!!!!! OH MY GOSH!!!!!! OH MY GOSH!!!!!! OH MY GOSH!!!!!!

4

THE WORLD OF WINE & BEER

Too often dismissed as the most basic and simplest elements of a bartender's work, the delights of wines and beers can expand into numerous other areas. Which is not to say that an aromatic glass of red wine or a frosty mug of beer are not satisfactory in their own right; quite to the contrary, it is with good reason that the bartender spends most of her time filling glasses with these drinking staples. Still, a number of creative approaches to these alcohols allow for some bold innovations that highlight just how profound and powerful they can be. This chapter attempts to do some justice to beers and wines by exploring their variations and by examining the mixed drinks that they can produce.

WINE & CHAMPAGNE

WINE, n. Fermented grape-juice known to the Women's Christian Union as "liquor," sometimes as "rum." Wine, madam, is God's next best gift to man.
—Ambrose Bierce, *Devil's Dictionary*

The first thing that you should know about wine is this: a lot of connoisseurs are extremely pompous, snooty people. If you find yourself in a conversation with one of these people and can't immediately name the three best years for Bordeaux wines in the last century, you may very well be sniffed at mercilessly.

Do not, however, let this deter you. Despite what the experts would like you to believe, you do not need to know a lot about wine to enjoy it. Serious wine appreciation can involve a staggering amount of detail, and it would take a lifetime (and certainly not just one chapter of a book) to affect knowledge of all the subtleties; however, a few basics—the different types of grapes and the different wine-growing regions, for example—are all you'll need to know to purchase and enjoy wine intelligently.

As you begin to experiment with different wines, remember which wines you like best. Wine appreciation is subjective, and when you know what you like, you'll be able to choose accordingly in almost any situation. Prices are not always the best indicators of quality—it's entirely possible to find a $7 bottle of wine that you like just as much as one that costs 10 times that amount. To find a good wine at a reasonable price, look for sales and ask wine store clerks for advice whenever you have questions.

Wines are classified as still, sparkling, or fortified. Still wines are non-carbonated beverages containing 7-15% alcohol. The three basic kinds of still wine are red, white, and rosé. Sparkling wines, such as champagne, sparkling burgundy, and Asti Spumante, may also be red, white, or rosé, with 7-15% alcohol, but they are all bubbly. Fortified wines, such as port and sherry, contain brandy, which brings the alcohol content up to a fortitudinous 18-22%. Dubonnet and vermouth have other flavorings added as well as brandy and are called "aromatics" or "apéritifs."

Most common wines are still. Interestingly enough, their red, white, or rose color does not indicate the color of the grapes from whence they came, but instead the length of time that the grape skins stayed in the wine during fermentation.

Aside from color, wines are classified according to their place of origin, grape variety, and vintage year. All of this information is contained on the wine label if it's not, you're probably dealing with a very cheap bottle. Vintage is less important to novice wine drinkers than the place of origin and the grape variety.

Wine is made all over the world in an ever increasing number of countries.Some of the largest wine-producing countries are the United States, France, Germany, Italy, Portugal, Spain, Chile, Australia, South Africa, and Japan. Japanese wine, called sake, is made from rice instead of grapes. Within most of these countries are a large variety of wine-producing regions, and wines frequently take their name from the region in which they're produced. For example, chablis is a white wine from the Chablis region in France, while burgundy is a red wine from the Burgundy region. Wine makers will occasionally take liberties with these designations—many American wines are known as chablis despite the fact that they are produced in the United States.

Many wines, including all of those produced in California, are referred to by the names of varieties of grapes, provided that the wine contains at least 51% of a certain grape. Some common "varietal" white wines include, from driest to sweetest, chardonnay, fumé blanc, riesling, and sauterne. White zinfandel is a sweet white wine made from red zinfandel grapes, which lends it a pinkish color. Common red varietals include zinfandel, pinot noir, merlot, and cabernet sauvignon.

In the United States, white wine outsells red and rosé by about 5 to 1. If you're stocking a bar on a limited budget, buy white. Dry to medium white wines meet with more universal approval than sweet wines, which make some drinkers queasy.

In storage, keep wine bottles on their sides so that the corks will stay moist, and protect them from temperature and light. As a general rule, serve red wine at room temperature and white wine chilled. If you're serving wine with food, tradition dictates that red wines go well with beef, pork, and lamb, while whites are better suited to poultry and fish, and vegetarians can drink whatever the hell they want.

WINE DRINKS

KIR

dash crème de cassis

dry white wine, chilled, to fill

Serve in a wine glass.

VERMOUTH

Vermouth is an apéritif named from the Latin "aperio" meaning "to open," in recognition of the fact that vermouth is supposed to excite the appetite and whet the palate before meals. The beverage is made from a neutral, dry white basic wine which is then infused with herbs and aromatic delights. While its Latin roots would seem to encourage a bottle of vermouth to be opened, one must needs take care to avoid skunking the beverage. The herbs dissipate once the bottle is opened unless it is re-capped tightly and refrigerated. Aged vermouth that is left to breathe outside a refrigerator will quickly become stale, losing its residency in the kingdom of Flavor Country.

SPRITZER

1 part white wine

1 part club soda

Serve on ice with a lemon twist in a large wine glass or tall, frosted highball glass.

VERMOUTH APÉRITIF

Serve sweet vermouth on ice with a lemon twist.

VERMOUTH COCKTAIL

1 oz. sweet vermouth

1 oz. dry vermouth

dash Angostura or orange bitters

Add ice, stir, and strain into a wineglass. Fill with soda water. Garnish with a cherry.

CHAMPAGNE DRINKS

ARISE MY LOVE
½ oz. green crème de menthe
champagne to fill

Serve in a champagne glass.

CARIBBEAN CHAMPAGNE
splash rum
splash crème de banane

Pour into a champagne glass. Add champagne to fill. Garnish with a banana slice.

CHAMPAGNE COCKTAIL
glass of champagne
2 dashes bitters
1 tsp. sugar

Stir without ice. Garnish with an extra-long spiral twist of lemon peel.

DIAMOND FIZZ
1½ oz. gin
1 oz. sour mix
1 tsp. sugar

Shake, strain into a highball glass with ice, and fill with champagne.

FRENCH 75
1 oz. gin
1 oz. sour mix
2 tsp. sugar

Shake with ice and strain over fresh ice into a highball or collins glass. Add champagne to fill. Garnish with an orange slice and a cherry.

KIR ROYALE
dash crème de cassis
chilled champagne to fill

Serve in a champagne glass.

MIMOSA

1 part champagne
1 part orange juice
dash triple sec (optional)

Garnish with an orange slice.

MIDORI MIMOSA

2 oz. Midori
2 tsp. lime juice
champagne to fill

Garnish with a lime wedge and strawberries (optional).

COOLERS

Serve these drinks over ice in tall, frosty glasses. At a busy bar, if a customer orders a wine cooler or spritzer, just pour about 3 oz. of wine over ice in a tall glass and fill with soda water. Since most coolers are made with wine or champagne, we've dumped the liqueur-based coolers into this section as well.

CHAMPAGNE COOLER

1 oz. brandy
1 oz. Cointreau or triple sec
champagne to fill

Garnish with mint sprigs.

COUNTRY CLUB COOLER

3 oz. dry vermouth
1 tsp. grenadine
soda water to fill

Garnish with an extra-long lemon spiral.

PINEAPPLE WINE COOLER

2½ oz. dry white wine
2½ oz. pineapple juice
½ tsp. powdered sugar
soda water to fill

Garnish with a lemon and an orange twist (extra-long spirals). As an option, add 1 oz. rum before you pour in the soda water.

RED WINE COOLER

3 oz. red wine

7-Up, Sprite, or soda water to fill

WHITE WINE COOLER

3 oz. white wine

7-Up, Sprite, or soda water to fill

APRICOT COOLER

1½ oz. apricot brandy

club soda or ginger ale to fill

BOSTON COOLER

2 oz. rum

2 oz. club soda

½ tsp. sugar

club soda or ginger ale to fill

Stir 2 oz. of club soda and sugar in a highball glass. Add rum and cracked ice, then fill with club soda or ginger ale. Garnish with lemon twist (extra-long spiral) and orange slice. This is a fizzier version of the Rum Collins.

GIN COOLER

2 oz. gin

2 oz. club soda

½ tsp. sugar

club soda or ginger ale to fill

Stir 2 oz. of club soda and sugar in a highball glass. Add gin and cracked ice, then fill with club soda or ginger ale. Garnish with lemon twist (extra-long spiral) and orange slice.

RUM COOLER

2 oz. light rum

2 oz. club soda

½ tsp. sugar

soda water or ginger ale to fill

Stir 2 oz. of club soda and sugar in a highball glass. Add rum and cracked ice, then fill with club soda or ginger ale. Garnish with lemon twist (extra-long spiral) and orange slice.

SCOTCH COOLER

2 oz. Scotch

splash crème de menthe

soda water to fill

DRINK CONTINUED ON THE NEST PAGE▶

Garnish with mint sprigs.

TEQUOOLER (TEQUILA COOLER)

1½ oz. tequila

juice of ½ lemon or lime

tonic water or soda water to fill

Garnish with a lemon twist (extra-long spiral).

VODKA COOLER

2 oz. vodka

2 oz. club soda

½ tsp. sugar

soda water or ginger ale to fill

Stir 2 oz. of club soda and sugar in a highball glass. Add vodka and cracked ice, then fill with club soda or ginger ale. Garnish with lemon twist (extra-long spiral) and orange slice.

BEER

While wine aficionados may argue the point, beer is probably the oldest of all alcoholic beverages. Over the years, the world has accumulated a lot of different brands of beer; however, all beers are brewed in much the same way that they have been since those times when the hottest cocktail parties in town were held inside of a pyramid.

1. MALT PREPARATION: The brewer steeps barley (other carbohydrates may be used, but barley is most common) in water and heats it to begin the beer-making process. This step imparts color and taste to the beer; depending on the degree of roasting, the final product will be either pale and light or dark and robust.

2. MASHING: Mashing involves a rather complicated process for preparing the malted barley. The malt enzymes break down the starch to sugar and the complex protein of the malt to simpler nitrogen compounds.

3. LAUTERING: the brewer removes spent grains and continues brewing the liquid.

4. BOILING AND HOPPING: The liquid is poured into huge kettles and boiled for about two hours, during which time hops are added to the brew. Hops, the dried flower cones of the hop vine, give beer a sharp, bitter flavor, which is a nice balance to the sweetness of malt sugars. Hops also contribute a pleasant aroma to the brew and help to preserve freshness. This unfermented mixture of malted barley and hops is called the wort.

5. HOPS SEPARATION AND COOLING: After the wort has taken on the flavor of the hops, they are removed and the brew passes through a cooling device.

6. FERMENTATION: The wort is transferred to fermenting vessels, and yeast is added. The yeast, which consists of living, single-celled fungi, takes the sugar in the brew and breaks it down into carbon dioxide and alcohol. The brewer can use two species of yeast and, depending on which he chooses, produce ale or lager.

7. STORAGE: After fermentation, the beer is cooled and placed in storage for at least two to four weeks.

8. PACKAGING: The beer is bottled and passes through a pasteurizer where the temperature of the beer is raised as high as 140°F to kill the yeast, then cooled to room temperature. The bottles are then capped and sold.

The word "beer" generally covers both ale and lager (and, if you believe what you see on The Simpsons, every other beverage in Australia), although most people use it specifically as a synonym for lager. Both products undergo basically the same brewing process, but a few variations account for the distinctly different tastes of the two.

LAGER is brewed at relatively low temperatures (around 131°F) using a "bottom-fermenting" yeast, meaning a yeast that works mostly from the bottom of the barrel. The brewer then draws the lager off the top, leaving the yeast in the tank. Most popular, mass-produced American beers are lagers. By contrast, ale is brewed at higher temperatures (around 140°F) using a "top-fermenting" yeast—a yeast that floats on top of the brew during fermentation and then must be skimmed off. Ale tastes hoppier (more bitter) than lager and has a higher alcohol content (4.4% to 5.5%, as opposed to lager's 3.2% to 4.5%). Popular ales include Molson Golden, Ballantine, and Bass.

PILSNER beer (such as Pilsner Urquell) is a kind of lager beer named for the famous brews of Pilsen in the Czech Republic. As a bartender, you will serve a lot of "light" Pilsners (Miller Lite, Amstel Light), which were brewed with extra enzymes and therefore have lower caloric, carbohydrate, and alcohol contents. Light beers contain 68 to 134 calories per 12 oz. (other beers have 150 to 180 calories) and 2.5% to 3.2% alcohol.

PORTER AND STOUT are sweet, dark, brown ales. Stout (such as Guinness) tastes slightly hoppier than porter (narrangansett, Anchor), has a thicker texture, and contains 5% to 6% alcohol.

MALT LIQUOR (Colt 45, King Cobra) is a lager that has a higher alcohol content than other lagers (over 5%). It tastes hoppier than beer, yet lighter than ale (actually, it tastes pretty gross...unless you're an expert malt licka picka).

BOCK beer (such as Genesee Bock) is a sweet, heavy, amber-to-dark colored lager beer containing 3.5% alcohol.

Unlike many wines and a few people, beer does not get better with age—in fact, beer keeps poorly. Bottled beer has a peak life expectancy of only six months, canned beer half that time, and kegs (which are unpasteurized) only one month. Keep this in mind when you see amazing beer sales—any time you see a beer priced considerably lower than it ought to be, it's a safe bet that it's getting skunky. This does not mean that it's not drinkable; however, you should resist the urge to stock up on huge quantities of beer that will probably start to turn on you in a couple of weeks.

Beer is sensitive to temperature extremes and to light, so store it in a cool, dark area—your refrigerator, for example. The ideal temperature is somewhere between 40 and 60 degrees Fahrenheit. At higher temperatures, the ingredients break down and the aroma and flavor deteriorate, resulting in "skunked beer." When frozen, the solids separate from the liquid and form flakes that do not go back into the solution when the beer thaws.

To serve the perfect beer, start with a sparkling clean glass dipped in cold water. You should keep special glasses just for beer; a film on the glass—from milk or detergent, for example—can alter the taste of the beer. For a thick, foamy head, pour the beer straight down the middle of the glass from about one inch above the rim. For a smaller head, tilt the glass and pour down the side. Then, before it is completely filled, bring it upright.

BEER DRINKS

Are you the kind of connoisseur whose favorite cocktail is a beer straight from the can? You'll be amazed at what you can do with your old standby—and we're not just talking about shotgunning it. Serve the following drinks in a beer mug or Pilsner glass. If you are serving from a keg of beer and have no idea how to use the pressure tap, see p. 126.

BLACK VELVET
1 part porter or stout
1 part champagne (extra dry)

Pour these carefully down the side of the glass to make two distinct layers. In all, 10 to 16 oz.

HALF-AND-HALF
1 part ale
1 part porter or stout

In all, 10 to 16 oz.

SHANDY GAFF
1 part beer
1 part ginger ale

In all, 10 to 16 oz.

BOILERMAKER
1 shot whiskey
1 mug full of beer

Add a jigger of whiskey to a mug of beer. You can (a) drink the whiskey and chase it with the beer (boring), (b) pour the shot into the beer (better), or (c) drop the shot—glass and all—into the mug of beer and chug it all down quickly before it foams all over you. This is sometimes called a "depth charge." Beer and whiskey, mighty risky!

HOP-SKIP-AND-GO-NAKED
1 oz. vodka

DRINK CONTINUED ON THE NEST PAGE▶

1 oz. gin

juice of ½ lime

beer to fill

Serve over ice. To serve as a punch, measure the ingredients by the bottle and case while using 12 limes.

BEER BUSTER

1½ oz. vodka

beer to fill

2 dashes Tabasco sauce

Stir lightly in a mug or Pilsner glass.

BLOODY BREW

1½ oz. vodka

2 oz. tomato juice

beer to fill

Serve in a mug or Pilsner glass.

SNAKEBITE

1 part beer

1 part cider

10-16 oz. total

This drink is a favourite of jolly olde England, and its mildly sweet flavor attests to the lack of vicious serpents in said land.

ROOT DOWN

1 shot root beer schnapps

beer

Fill a beer glass three-quarters full with beer, then drop in the shot of schnapps (for the gamut of possible techniques, refer to the Boiler-maker, above). In one single and dramatic quaffing gesture, down the entire concoction, which should taste just like root beer. The shot glass, however, does not taste like root beer—do not swallow glass!

NOVELTY DRINKS, PUNCHES, & NON-ALCOHOLIC ALTERNATIVES

WELCOME TO THE EXCITING WORLD OF NOVELTY DRINKS. NOVELTIES—FUNNY HATS, FLAMING SHOTS, LITTLE UMBRELLAS, AND FRUITY PUNCHES. IN OTHER WORDS, THINGS YOU MIGHT EXPECT WOULD BE ILLUSTRATED BY THE SAME ARTISTS WHO DO AIRBRUSHED JIM MORRISON T-SHIRTS AT THE STATE FAIR.

NOVELTY DRINKS ARE NEITHER FUNNY NOR LIGHTHEARTED, THEY ARE SIMPLY NOVEL.

THE CURSE OF NOVELTY IS TO BE EPHEMERAL.

SO, PLEASE ENJOY THESE NON-COPYRIGHTED PIECES OF VICTORIAN WOODCUTS ON THE FOLLOWING 20 PAGES.

HAPPY DRINKING!

NOVELTY DRINKS

Rarely ordered in a bar, novelty drinks provide an intriguing and un-usual change of pace. Both for their multifarious palate and the aes-thetic displays that often accompany them, novelty drinks can add an illusion (or the actuality) of refinement to your drink-making lexicon. Most of the beverages in this chapter prove delightful for special events, whether for private parties that you're hosting or for a quick recovery from seasonal chills. This chapter is divided into four categories: hot drinks, for picturesque moments of languid, wintry bliss; flaming drinks, for the dramatic bartender; punch recipes, for both conventional and unconventional means of serving the masses at a tasteful fête; and light and non-alcoholic drinks, because people who aren't getting liquored up deserve to enter Flavor Country, too.

HOT DRINKS

There's nothing like a piping hot drink on a cold day, a truth that gains even more validity when you add some booze for extra warmth. While not nearly as popular as the mixed drinks of the previous chapter, all of these potent concoctions can still get you completely snokkered with cheer. Most of these drinks specify an ingredient or two to be added to a non-alcoholic hot drink such as coffee, cider, or tea. For mixing purposes, assume that the serving size of that drink is what you would drink normally—about 5 to 8 oz. The drinks are listed alphabeti-cally for easy reference.

COFFEE DRINKS
BAILEY'S COFFEE
1½ oz. Bailey's Irish Cream
hot black coffee

Stir. Top with whipped cream.

CAFFÉ DI AMARETTO

1½ oz. amaretto

hot black coffee

Stir. Top with whipped cream.

CAFÉ MEXICANO

1 oz. Kahlúa

½ oz. tequila

hot black coffee

Stir. Garnish as desired.

IRISH COFFEE

1½ oz. Irish whiskey

1 tsp. sugar

hot black coffee

Stir. Top with whipped cream.

JAMAICAN COFFEE

1 oz. Tia Maria (or Kahlúa)

¾ oz. rum

hot coffee

Stir. Top with whipped cream, if desired, and dust with nutmeg.

KAHLÚA IRISH COFFEE

1 oz. Kahlúa

1 oz. Irish whiskey or Bailey's Irish Cream

hot black coffee

Stir. Garnish as desired.

KIOKI COFFEE

1 oz. Kahlúa

½ oz. brandy

hot black coffee

Stir. Garnish as desired.

MEXICAN COFFEE

1½ oz. Kahlúa

hot black coffee

Stir. Top with whipped cream, if desired, and dust with nutmeg or add a cinnamon stick. Tequila can also be either substituted for or combined with the Kahlúa.

NUTTY COFFEE
1 oz. amaretto
½ oz. Frangelico
hot black coffee

Stir. Top with whipped cream.

NUTTY IRISHMAN COFFEE
1 oz. Irish cream or Irish whiskey
1 oz. Frangelico
hot black coffee

Top with whipped cream and sprinkle with chocolate shavings.

ROMAN COFFEE
1½ oz. Galliano
hot black coffee

Stir. Top with whipped cream.

OTHER HOT DRINKS

CHIMNEY FIRE
1½ oz. amaretto
hot cider

Garnish with a cinnamon stick. Chimney Fires can burn ever so brightly in a multitude of colors. For other flavors, just substitute Southern Comfort or dark rum for amaretto. To burn your whole house down, drink a lot of these.

COMFORT MOCHA
1½ oz. Southern Comfort
1 tsp. instant cocoa or hot chocolate
1 tsp. instant coffee

Add boiling water. Top with whipped cream if desired.

GOOD NIGHT
2 oz. rum
1 tsp. sugar
warm milk

Serve in a mug. Dust with nutmeg.

GROG

1½ oz. rum
1 tsp. sugar
juice of ¼ lemon
boiling water

Serve in a mug.

HOT BUTTERED RUM

2 oz. rum
1 tsp. sugar
1 tsp. butter
boiling water

Dust with nutmeg.

HOT GOLD

3 oz. amaretto
6 oz. very warm orange juice

Garnish with a cinnamon stick.

HOT TODDY

2 oz. whiskey
1 tsp. sugar
boiling water

Serve in a mug. Garnish with a lemon slice and dust with nutmeg or add cinnamon stick.

HOT WINE LEMONADE

1½ oz. red wine
juice of ½-1 lemon
1½ tsp. sugar
boiling water

Garnish with a lemon twist.

AMARETTO TEA

1½ oz. amaretto
1 tsp. sugar (optional)
hot tea

Do not stir the amaretto. Top with whipped cream.

NOVELTY ITEM 1:
THE PRINTING PRESS

The printing press was developed in 1925 by a team of European and American scientists, working together as part of a global consortium on the lack of appropriate means of typographic dissemination. The work was very difficult, however, and it took over three years before a working prototype was developed. In fact, by the time there was a model ready to go into mass production, many of the men who worked on the original designs had already passed on—unable to see the radical fruition of their fragile dream. Today, few people know this important history. Unfortunately, few people know just how lucky they are to live in a society where the printed word is as free as air, where ideas are the common currency, and the fellowship of humankind can be united under the vermillion banner of cheap, reproducible art. Prior to 1925, few opportunities existed for the entreprenurial student of letters—to write and distribute a book like this Official Harvard Student Agencies Bartending Course Book would have taken many lifetimes of cloistered monks, illuminating their rubricked quires by Matins candlelight. Dristribution in the 19th and early 20th Century was still handled by trusted oxcarts, and the dusty cowboys who drove them.

1

☐☐☐☐☐☐☐☐☐
FLAMING

Nothing says "U!S!A!" quite as dramatically as explosives on the Fourth of July. Sometimes, however, pyrotechnic fervor on this magnificent day takes on different, more inventive dimensions, potentially including the lighting of flaming drinks. If you learn nothing else from this guide, keep this in mind: DON'T FLAME YOUR DRINKS NEAR FIRE-WORKS. A failure to heed this warning will dramatically increase the likelihood that the bombs won't just be bursting in air. And that's not what the Fourth of July is about.

KAHLÚA AND HOT CHOCOLATE

1 oz. Kahlúa

hot chocolate

Top with whipped cream.

TOM AND JERRY

1 egg, separated

2 tsp. sugar

¼ cup hot milk

1 tbsp. butter

1½ oz. rum

Heat the milk and butter together until hot. Beat the egg white and egg yolk separately, then add the egg white to the yolk and beat in the sugar. Put the mixture in a warm mug and fill with rum and more hot milk, then stir. Float ½ oz. brandy on top . Dust with nutmeg.

FLAME DRINKS

Flaming drinks can be a lot of fun when done safely and correctly. They are much less fun if they accidentally result in asomeone's hair lighting on fire (or worse...). To flame a drink, first warm only one teaspoon of the required liquor over a match flame, then ignite. Once it is lit, carefully pour it over the prepared recipe. Stand back! This method is usually safer than lighting the liquor right in the glass.

BLUE BLAZER

2½ oz. whiskey

2½ oz. boiling water

1 tbsp. honey (optional)

☐☐☐☐☐☐☐☐☐
BLUE BLAZER

Unlike Green Lantern, Black Vulcan, the Green Hornet, Flash, and Darryl Dawkins (a.k.a. Chocolate Thunder), the Blue Blazer is not a superhero. Nevertheless, those who correctly prepare this concoction in the dark (with great care, of course) will become a bartending superhero, as the mixing process will appear like a juggling act of liquid, blue fire.

Pour the whiskey and the boiling water into two separate mugs. Ignite the whiskey. Mix by pouring back and forth several times between the two mugs. Garnish with a lemon twist and serve in a warm on-the-rocks glass. Add honey if desired.

SOUTHERN BLAZER

1½ oz. Southern Comfort

1 oz. Kahlúa

2½ oz. boiling water

1 tbsp. honey (optional)

Pour the alcohol and the boiling water into two sepa-

rate mugs. Ignite the booze. Mix by pouring back and forth several times between the two mugs. Garnish with a lemon twist and serve in a warm on-the-rocks glass. Add honey if desired.

BRANDY BLAZER

2 oz. brandy

1 tsp. sugar

1 piece orange peel

1 lemon twist

Put ingredients in an Old Fashioned or rocks glass. Ignite. Stir with a bar spoon, then strain into a thick, stemmed glass.

CAFÉ ROYALE

1 cube of sugar soaked in brandy

1 cup of hot black coffee

Ignite sugar in a spoon and drop into the coffee as it caramelizes and the flame dies out. Float cream on top.

HARBOR LIGHT

½ oz. Kahlúa

½ oz. tequila

½ oz. 151-proof rum

Layer the ingredients in a shot glass, then ignite.

LIGHTHOUSE

2 oz. Galliano

2 oz. dry vermouth

Ignite Galliano in a shot glass and pour it over dry vermouth in a cocktail glass. This drink may be served on the rocks in a champagne glass and garnished with a lemon slice.

PUNCH RECIPES

So you're a little shy about pouring in public? Try some of these punch recipes so that you can show off your new bartending abilities while still mixing in the comforts and privacy of your own home. All of the following recipes should be served from a punch bowl with a large block of ice in it, unless directions specify otherwise. For each serving, ladle about 4 oz. into a plastic lowball glass.

BRANDY PUNCH

juice of 12 lemons

juice of 4 oranges

DRINK CONTINUED ON THE NEST PAGE▶

sugar
1 cup grenadine
1 cup triple sec
2 liters brandy
2 cups tea (optional)
1 quart soda water

Mix the lemon and orange juice, add sugar to taste, then mix with all the other ingredients. Add soda water just before serving. Garnish with fruit. Yields 35 to 50 servings.

BUDDHA PUNCH

1 bottle Rhine wine
½ cup curaçao
1 cup rum
1 cup orange juice
1 quart soda water
Angostura bitters to taste
1 bottle chilled champagne

Add champagne just before serving. Garnish with mint leaves and fruit slices. One bottle of champagne usually contains 750 mL or one quart. Either size is acceptable. Yields 25 to 30 servings.

CANADIAN FRUIT PUNCH

2 liters Canadian whiskey
12 oz. can frozen orange juice concentrate
12 oz. can frozen lemonade concentrate
12 oz. can frozen pineapple juice concentrate
1 cup simple syrup (for the recipe, see page 24)
3 quarts strong iced tea

Garnish with fruit. Yields 65 to 75 servings.

CLARET PUNCH

2 bottles claret (or a 1½ liter bottle)
1 cup triple sec
2 cups brandy
sugar to sweeten
juice of 12 lemons
2 quarts soda water

Add soda water just before serving. Yields about 40 servings.

EGGNOG

1 lb. confectioners' sugar

DRINK CONTINUED IN TWO PAGES▶

1

12 eggs, separated

1 pint brandy

1 pint light rum

1½ quarts milk

1 pint heavy cream

Beat confectioners' sugar in with egg yolks. Stir in slowly: brandy, rum, milk, and cream. Chill. Fold in stiffly beaten egg whites before serving—don't beat or stir the whites. Do not serve with ice. Sprinkle nutmeg on top. Yields 45 to 65 servings.

FISH HOUSE PUNCH

juice of 12 lemons

powdered sugar

1 liter rum

1 bottle brandy (750 mL)

½ cup peach brandy

2-3 quarts cola, flavored soda, or lemonade

Add enough sugar to sweeten the lemons. Add soda just before serving. Garnish with citrus fruits. Yields 25 to 35 servings.

FRENCH CREAM PUNCH

1 cup amaretto

1 cup Kahlúa or coffee brandy

¼ cup triple sec

½ gallon softened vanilla ice cream

No ice. Mix well. Yields 15 to 20 servings.

FRUIT PUNCH

1 liter vodka

1 bottle white wine

2 12 oz. cans frozen fruit juice concentrate (pineapple, grapefruit, or orange)

2 quarts soda water

Add soda water just before serving. Yields about 40 servings.

GIN PUNCH

2 liters gin

1 pint lemon juice

2 cups cranberry juice cocktail

1 quart orange juice

½ cup grenadine

1 quart soda water

Add soda water just before serving. Garnish with sprigs of mint. Yields about 45 servings.

GREEN MACHINE

2 liters vodka

1 12 oz. can frozen limeade concentrate

½ pint lemon sherbert

½ pint lime sherbert

Yields about 35 servings.

HOT APPLE RUM PUNCH

1 liter dark rum

1 quart apple cider

2 or 3 cinnamon sticks, broken

1½ tbsp. butter

Heat in saucepan until almost boiling. Serve hot. Yields about 15 servings.

HOT MULLED WINE

3 cups water

2 cinnamon sticks, whole

8 cloves

peel of 1 lemon, cut into twists or into one long spiral

1 cup sugar

1 bottle dry red wine

Boil everything except the wine in a large saucepan for 10 minutes, then add the wine. Heat but do not allow to boil. Just before serving add a splash of brandy and a lemon slice to each glass. Serve hot. Yields 15 to 25 servings.

OOGIE PRINGLE PUNCH

1 liter rum

1 quart pineapple juice

1 quart cranberry juice

Garnish with lemon slices. Yields about 25 servings.

PARTY PUNCH

2 cups sugar

1 cup water

2 cups concentrated fruit syrup

1 cup lemon juice

2 cups orange juice

DRINK CONTINUED ON THE NEST PAGE▶

2 cups pineapple juice
2 bottles chilled champagne
2 quarts ginger ale
1 quart soda water

Boil the sugar and water for five minutes, then add all the fruity good-
ness (syrup and the juices). Just before serving, add the champagne,
ginger ale, and soda water.

PLANTER'S PUNCH

1 liter rum
1 pint Jamaican rum (Myers's)
1 pint fresh lime juice
1 pint simple syrup (for the recipe, see page 36)
1 quart soda water

Add soda water just before serving. Garnish with orange slices and
cherries. Yields about 30 servings.

PLANTER'S PUNCH (VARIATION)

1 liter rum
1 cup Jamaican rum (Myers's)
1 cup curaçao (optional)
1 pint lemon juice
1 cup orange juice
1 cup pineapple juice

Garnish with orange slices and cherries. Yields about 20 servings.

RED WINE PUNCH

2 bottles dry red wine
1 pint lemon juice
1 cup simple syrup (for the recipe, see page 36)
1 cup raspberry syrup
2 quarts soda water

Add soda water just before serving. Yields about 40 servings.

RUM FRUIT PUNCH

1½ liters rum
½ pineapple, sliced
1 pint strawberries
¾ cup simple syrup (for the recipe, see page 36)
1 cup lemon juice
2 cups pineapple juice
1 pint thinly sliced strawberries

2 quarts soda water

Chill everything except the strawberries and soda water for two hours. Just before serving, add the strawberries and soda water.

SANGRÍA

2 bottles rosé wine
3 oz. curaçao or triple sec
2 oz. brandy
1 cup orange juice
½ cup lemon juice
¼ cup sugar
1 liter club soda
30 oz. can fruit cocktail
3 sliced oranges

Just before serving, add the soda water. Then garnish amply with fruit. Yields 35 to 40 servings.

SANGRÍA MARIA

1½ liters hearty burgundy wine
1 quart ginger ale
4 oranges sliced into wedges
2 lemons sliced into wedges
2 peaches sliced into wedges
any other fruits you wish to add

Let stand for at least two hours. Strain into punch bowl with ice. Garnish with lemon slices, orange slices, and cherries. Yields about 25 servings.

NARRI'S SANGRÍA

2 cups dark rum

1 quart sweet red wine

1 quart dry red wine

This delicious recipe comes from the bar of Narri, a former manager of the Harvard Bartending Course. Soak cut-up fruit (strawberries, oranges, lemons, limes, and whatever you like) overnight in the rum. Then add the wines before serving. Yields 25 to 30 servings.

SOUTHERN COMFORT PUNCH

1 bottle Southern Comfort (750 mL)

2 cups grapefruit juice

1 cup lemon juice

2 quarts 7-Up, Sprite, or ginger ale

Yields about 30 servings.

SPARKLING PINK PUNCH

1 bottle chilled champagne

1 bottle rosé wine

1 10 oz. container thawed whole frozen raspberries or strawberries

Pour the champagne and wine over the fruit. Yields about 15 servings.

SUPERSONIC NOG

1 liter Kahlúa

1 liter vodka

4 quarts prepared dairy egg nog

Dust with nutmeg or cinnamon. Yields about 40 servings.

TEQUILA PUNCH

1 liter tequila

3 liters sauterne

2 quarts fruit cubes and balls (8 cups)

1 bottle chilled champagne

Sweeten to taste. Add champagne just before serving. Yields about 45 servings.

TROPICAL PUNCH

5 bottles white wine

1 lb. brown sugar

1 quart orange juice

1 pint lemon juice

5 sliced bananas

1 pineapple, cut or chopped

3 liters light rum

1 pint dark rum

2 cups crème de banane

Blend the wine, sugar, juices, and fruits. Cover and let stand overnight. Add the rums and crème de banane before straining into a punch bowl over ice. Garnish with fruits. Yields about 100 servings.

VELVET HAMMER PUNCH

1 bottle sauterne

12 oz. apricot brandy

1 liter vodka

1 bottle chilled champagne

1 quart ginger ale

Add champagne and ginger ale just before serving. Yields about 30 servings.

WEDDING PUNCH

1 liter vodka

3 cups orange juice

1 cup lemon juice

2 quarts ginger ale

Garnish with cherries, lemons, and orange slices. Yields about 35 servings.

WELDER'S PUNCH

1 liter vodka

1 quart ginger ale, 7-Up, or Sprite

1 quart fruit punch

1 quart orange juice

Garnish with orange slices and cherries. Yields about 35 servings.

WHISKEY PUNCH

2 liters bourbon

½ cup curaçao

1 quart apple juice

juice of 6 lemons

2 oz. grenadine

4 quarts ginger ale

Add ginger ale just before serving. Garnish with cherries. Yields 60 to 65 servings.

WINE PUNCH

1½ lbs. sugar
2 quarts soda water
2 bottles dry red wine
1 pint brandy
1 pint rum
1 bottle sparkling white wine

Dissolve the sugar in the soda water before adding the red wine, brandy, and rum. Before serving, add the sparkling white wine. Garnish with sliced oranges and pineapple slices. Yields 45 to 50 servings.

CHAMPAGNE PUNCHES

CHAMPAGNE PUNCH

2 or 3 bottles chilled champagne
½ cup curaçao
½ cup lemon juice
1 quart soda water
½ lb. confectioners' sugar

Mix this punch just before serving. Yields 25 to 35 servings.

CHAMPAGNE PUNCH (VARIATION)

½ cup brandy
½ cup Cointreau or triple sec
2 bottles chilled champagne

Yields about 15 servings.

CHAMPAGNE PUNCH (VARIATION)

½ cup light rum
½ cup dark rum
juice of 2 lemons
juice of 2 oranges
1 cup pineapple juice
½ cup sugar
2 bottles chilled champagne

Add champagne just before serving. Yields about 20 servings.

CHAMPAGNE PUNCH (VARIATION)

6 oranges
sugar
4 bottles champagne
1 bottle Mosel wine

Slice and arrange oranges on the bottom of a punch bowl. Sprinkle with sugar and add wine. Just before serving, place an ice block in the bowl and add chilled champagne. Yields about 30 servings.

CHAMPAGNE HOLIDAY PUNCH

1 bottle chilled champagne

2 quarts ginger ale

1 (8 oz.) can crushed pineapple with juice

1 quart raspberry sherbert

Mix this punch just before serving. Yields 25 to 35 servings.

CHAMPAGNE RUM PUNCH

2 liters rum

1 bottle sweet vermouth (750 mL)

1 quart orange juice

1 bottle chilled champagne

Add champagne just before serving. Garnish with sliced bananas. Yields about 40 servings.

CHAMPAGNE SHERBERT PUNCH

1 quart lemon or pineapple sherbert

2 bottles chilled champagne

1 bottle sauterne

Put sherbert in first. Garnish with lemon slices and/or pineapple chunks. Yields about 25 servings.

NON-ALCOHOLIC PUNCHES

CARDINAL PUNCH

2 quarts cranberry juice

1 quart orange juice

juice of 4 lemons

8 bottles ginger ale

Add ginger ale just before serving over ice.

FRUIT JUICE COMBO

1 cup tomato juice

1 cup V-8 (or other vegetable juice)

1 cup apple juice

1 cup cranberry juice

1 cup grapefruit juice

1 cup lemonade

DRINK CONTINUED ON THE NEST PAGE▶

1 cup orange juice
1 cup pineapple juice
8 drops Tabasco sauce

Garnish with a skewer of fresh pineapple, orange, and apple slices with which to stir. Serve over ice in a highball glass. Makes eight servings.

FRUIT PUNCH

36 oz. water
1 12 oz. can frozen grape juice concentrate
1 12 oz. can frozen lemonade concentrate
1 12 oz. can frozen orange juice concentrate
1 quart ginger ale
1 pint raspberry sherbert

Mix the water and concentrate. Add ginger ale before serving, then spoon the sherbert over the punch.

KENTUCKY DERBY

1½ cups sugar
2 cups cold water
1 cup lemon juice
2 quarts ginger ale

Garnish with lemon slices and mint sprigs.

LONG ISLAND TALL BOY

6 oz. can lemonade concentrate
1 quart orange juice

Garnish with strawberries and lime slices. Makes four to eight servings.

RED ROOSTER PUNCH

4 cups V-8 (or other vegetable juice)
10 oz. ginger ale
1 tbsp. lime juice
1 tsp. Worcestershire sauce
dash tabasco sauce

Makes about six servings.

SNOOPY PUNCH

1 12 oz. can frozen lemonade concentrate
1 12 oz. can frozen fruit punch concentrate

1 pint pineapple sherbert
3 lemons, sliced
1 quart ginger ale

Add ginger ale just before serving. If you serve this punch to anyone over 12, you may want to give it a different name. Something tough. Like No Limit Gangsta Punch.

STRAWBERRY ANGEL

1 pint fresh strawberries
1 13½ oz. can sweetened, condensed milk
Blend with ice and serve in lowball glasses.

sunset
3 cups V-8 (or other vegetable juice)
½ tsp. horseradish
½ tsp. Worcestershire sauce

Makes four servings.

UNREAL CHAMPAGNE

1 cup sugar
2 cups water
2 cups grapefruit juice
juice of 1 lemon
2 28 oz. bottles of ginger ale
dash grenadine

Add ginger ale just before serving. Serve in champagne glasses. Makes 15 to 20 servings.

PUNCH ALTERNATIVES

If you aren't thrilled with any of these punch recipes, try converting your favorite highball into punch form. For example, a Seabreeze contains:

> 1½ oz. vodka
> 2 oz. grapefruit juice (approximately)
> 2 oz. cranberry juice (approximately)

In punch form, this would loosely translate to:
> 1 liter vodka
> 2 quarts grapefruit juice
> 2 quarts cranberry juice

This recipe would make a beautiful, delicious, cool summer punch.

Adapt the ingredients to suit your tastes—add more mixer or vodka to vary the alcohol content.

LIGHT & NON-ALCOHOLIC DRINKS

Even without alcohol, many of these concoctions are very tasty and should be an option at any party. As a responsible bartender, a non-alcoholic drink is a necessity that can be used not only to quench the thirst of non-drinkers, but may also be an integral tool when deciding to cut someone off. In the past few years, non-alcoholic beers and wines have become increasingly popular and are a definite plus to have around when bartending. The selection of these drinks is constantly increasing and gives non-drinkers and designated drivers even more alternatives to drinking.

The term "light alcoholic" in the heading warrants further explanation. Many mixers such as bitters and extracts may contain alcohol, and great care should be taken in their use. Certain people may have strong physiological reactions to even the smallest amounts of alcohol, so a responsible bartender should be aware of exactly what is going into a "non-alcoholic" drink.

There is an infinite number of combinations of fruit juices that can create potable beverages. Also, many popular drinks can be converted to their "virgin" counterparts simply by eliminating the alcohol in them. Once again, don't be afraid to experiment—you may just invent a popular new drink.

BEACH BLANKET BINGO
4 oz. cranberry juice
4 oz. grape juice
club soda to fill

Garnish with a lime wedge and serve over ice in a highball glass.

CRANBERRY COOLER
2 oz. cranberry juice
juice of ½ lime
soda water to fill

Serve over ice in a highball glass.

FRITZER
1 tsp. sugar
2 dashes bitters
soda water to fill

Garnish with a lemon twist. Please note that some bitters contain small amounts of alcohol and may be harmful to some non-drinkers.

GRAPEBERRY

4 oz. cranberry juice

4 oz. grapefruit juice

Garnish with a lime wedge. Serve in a highball glass over ice.

INNOCENT PASSION

4 oz. passion fruit juice

splash cranberry juice

splash orange juice

juice of ½ lemon

soda water to fill

Serve over ice in a highball glass.

LIME COLA

juice of ½ lime

cola to fill

Serve over ice in a highball glass.

MICKEY MOUSE

1 scoop vanilla ice cream

cola to fill

Top with whipped cream and two cherries to give the effect of a silly-looking mouse without having to get ripped off in Orlando. Serve with a straw and a long-handled spoon.

PINK SNOWMAN

1 cup orange juice

1 10 oz. package frozen strawberries

2 large scoops vanilla ice cream

Blend and serve with another scoop of vanilla ice cream.

ROY ROGERS

dash grenadine

cola to fill

Garnish with a cherry.

SHIRLEY TEMPLE

dash grenadine

7-Up or Sprite to fill

Garnish with a cherry.

UNFUZZY NAVEL
4 oz. peach nectar
4 oz. orange juice
juice of ½ lemon
dash grenadine

Shake and serve over fresh ice in a highball glass. Garnish with an orange slice.

VANILLA COLA
splash of vanilla extract
cola to fill

Serve over ice in a highball glass. Vanilla extract frequently contains a small amount of alcohol and may be harmful to some non-drinkers.

VIRGIN COLADA
4-6 oz. coconut cream
4-6 oz. pineapple juice
Blend with ice. Garnish with a cherry and a pineapple chunk and serve in a highball glass.

VIRGIN MARY
tomato juice to ¾ full
small splash lemon juice
dash Worcestershire sauce
dash Tabasco (more for a hotter drink)
shake of salt and pepper
¼ tsp. horseradish (optional)

6

THE COCKTAIL PARTY

THE COCKTAIL PARTY

Cocktail parties are like relationships—they can be extremely satisfying, an utter nightmare, or somewhere in between. Unlike relationships, however, the right combination of people isn't always enough to guarantee a good cocktail party. While it's true that a roomful of rotten human beings will usually make for a bad time in any situation, even a party full of your closest friends could turn sour if you fail to plan properly.

Good cocktail party planning involves four steps: buying the right supplies, setting it up, keeping the bar supplied as the party progresses, and knowing when and how to throw everyone out. If you follow each step properly, things should go smoothly. At the very least, if you've planned a good party, you can feel free to blame anything that goes wrong on bad luck. Or bad guests.

Guests are actually the single most important factor in planning and running a party. At almost every step, what you need to do varies according to the kind of party you're having—and the kind of guests you're inviting. For example, if you're having 30 nuns over for drinks, you'll want to buy very different supplies than if you invited the same number of marines. By the same token, if you're planning a 20-keg fraternity party, you'll want to set up the bar (or bars) differently than you would for Uncle Phil's retirement party. (Obviously, this depends on what kind of person your Uncle Phil is. But you get the point.) Just keep in mind that you're trying to maximize your guests' enjoyment, and adjust accordingly.

STEP 1: GETTING THE RIGHT SUPPLIES

This is probably the most important step in putting together a successful party. Your guests will forgive you if you put the vodka in the wrong place on the bar or forget to refill the peanut dish, but if you run out of liquor 45 minutes into a three-hour party, you're not going to make anyone very happy. Although the exact items you may need vary considerably depending on the party, there are certain basic items—liquor, beer, mixers, ice, etc.—that you will need to have on hand for any occasion. Once again, keep your guests in mind as you decide what you'll need.

First, you have to decide what kinds of drinks you would like to serve. The basic cocktail bar includes the following:

☐ **AT LEAST TWO KINDS OF LIGHT ALCOHOL:** gin and vodka (usually rum as well and sometimes tequila—especially if any Texans will be in attendance).

☐ **AT LEAST TWO KINDS OF DARK ALCOHOL:** Scotch and bourbon (usually also blended whiskey).

☐ **TWO VERMOUTHS:** dry and sweet.

☐ **WINE:** white and red (possibly also rosé and fortified wines like port or sherry).

☐ **BEER**

☐ **A SELECTION OF NON-ALCOHOLIC DRINKS.**

FIVE VARIABLES WILL INFLUENCE YOUR LIQUOR DECISIONS:

SEASON: In warm weather, people tend to order light alcohols, beer, and white wine. Conversely, in winter, stock up on dark alcohols, coffee drinks (such as Irish coffee and Mexican coffee), sherry, brandy, and red wine.

AGE: Younger people usually prefer light alcohol, blended drinks, wine, beer, and sweet-tasting liqueur cocktails. Older guests drink more dark alcohols, usually unmixed. Buy the highest quality, most prestigious brands you can afford for older, whiskey-drinking guests. They will recognize and expect better names.

HOLIDAYS, THEMES, AND SPECIAL OCCASIONS: If the party theme or a holiday season lends itself to special drinks, alter your bar's offerings accordingly. Serve eggnog, hot mulled wine, or punch at a Christmas party; champagne on New Year's Eve; mint juleps on Kentucky Derby Day; green-colored beer on St. Patrick's Day; a red or pink "love potion" punch on Valentine's Day. If your boss is indicted for embezzling funds and has to flee to Mexico, serve margaritas at his going-away party. He probably won't be able to attend, but he would no doubt appreciate the gesture.

TIME OF DAY: At a 10 a.m. brunch bar, don't expect to be making many Zombies, or even gin and tonics. Instead, concentrate on mimosas, screwdrivers, and Bloody Marys. Before dinner, serve light apéritifs—drinks to stimulate appetites, not anesthesize them: for instance, wine, light cocktails, Dubonnet, and Kir. As a general rule, add more liquor and more variety as the day progresses, culminating with a fully stocked bar for the 8 p.m. to 2 a.m. crowd.

GUESTS' PREFERENCES: Use your own judgment for other bar adjustments. If your best friend drinks only Sombreros, keep a bottle of Kahlúa at the bar.

LIQUOR

For a typical four-hour cocktail party, buy one liter of hard alcohol for every six guests. Feel free to adjust according to the drinking habits of your guests. Make sure you buy the one-liter size because it's easier to handle; larger bottles may cost less per drink, but they are bulky, heavy, and often won't take speedpourers. Also, unless you're giving an informal party at home, think twice about buying large bottles and pouring the liquor into smaller containers—this "marrying" of bottles is illegal in many states. You will need only one bottle of each vermouth.

Give a reasonable amount of thought to brand-name selection. Two factors should govern which brands you buy: your budget and your desire to impress the guests. If you're financially secure and you're coordinating a party for the boss—or your future in-laws—buy premium liquor (the name brands considered the highest quality, and usually the most expensive). On a more limited budget for a party with the neighbors—or your current in-laws—you can get by with call brands (good, quality, recognizable brands, but usually cheaper than top shelf). For a fraternity party—or a party for your ex-in-laws—buy bottom-shelf or generic liquor. Remember that most students have very few qualms about drinking "Funky Town" vodka. If you're making punch, you can usually get away with using cheaper brands as long as you mix the punch well out of sight of your guests.

If you must economize, buy cheaper brands of light alcohols; they usually go into mixed drinks, so guests can't taste brand differences. Cutting corners here will allow you to spend more on the higher quality, dark alcohols, which people often drink unmixed. For a more extensive discussion of liquor quality and brand selection, see Chapter 1.

To save money without sacrificing name-brand prestige, consider mixing weaker drinks. Make a 1¼ oz. or a 1 oz. highball and the liquor bottles won't empty as quickly. Be careful, however—this may make your harder-drinking guests irate.

When you order for a large party, ask in advance at your local liquor store if you can buy on consignment, a deal that allows you to return any unopened, sealed bottles for a refund after the party. Some stores charge extra for this service, but in some situations it's worth the cost.

BEER

For a standard, four-hour cocktail party, plan on about one case of beer (24 beers) for every 10 guests. Keep in mind that younger crowds tend to drink much more beer than older ones, and the quality of beers differs even more widely than that of liquors. If you're having 35 guests or more, consider purchasing a quarter keg (about 7.8 gallons—the equivalent of more than three cases, or 83 12 oz. servings). For 70 guests, buy a keg (technically a half-keg, which contains 15½ gallons—about seven cases, or 165 12 oz. servings). Keg beer is economical in the long run, but you will have to leave a deposit on the keg and tap. For the best-tasting beer, move the keg to its party location at least four hours before the party and keep it consistently cold until empty. Put it in a big tub or barrel, pack chunks of ice around it (try for block ice, which won't melt as fast as cubed or cocktail ice), and cover it with a big plastic bag or towel.

Most kegs use a standard pressure-tap. Take hold of the two small outcropping handles attached to the ring at the base and turn counterclockwise. Then place the tap on the outlet and turn the ring clockwise to screw it into the keg. If you did not turn the ring far enough in the counterclockwise direction, you may find yourself soaked in beer. You can raise the pressure on the stream of beer flowing out by pumping the tap; you can lower the pressure by pulling on the small release pin at the base of the tap. The first few beers coming out of the keg will usually be very foamy. You will have to pump the tap periodically to keep a steady stream flowing as the level of beer in the keg decreases. A very small minority of taps work differently from this one; don't hesitate to ask for more information at the liquor store when you pick up the keg.

WINE

The amount and kind of wine you'll need varies from party to party. The heavy wine-drinking group (not to be confused with "winos"—a classification that connotes addling about in public while knocking back a paper bag full o' cheap wine) may consume three or more glasses per person, whereas an older crowd gathered during cold weather would drink only half a glass per person. One case (12 bottles) of wine contains about 60 servings. Generally speaking, younger crowds drink more than older crowds, although they also tend to be less picky—you might just be able to get away with that four-liter jug of red (something that you shouldn't attempt with a more sophisticated crowd). White wine is more popular in warmer weather, whereas fortified wines, reds, brandies, and sherry are more appropriate in the winter. It would take an entire book (not this one) to describe the endless varieties of wines available; ask for help at your liquor store or look for a slightly dry, inexpensive white wine.

Wine comes in bottles containing 750 mL, 1½ liters, and 3 liters, and occasionally even larger bottles. Buy whatever size costs the least. It is perfectly appropriate to transfer wine from large bottles to carafes for serving ease and attractiveness.

PUNCHES

For any gathering of 15 people or more, it might be easier to serve punch in addition to or even instead of other drinks. Punches are especially appropriate for the holiday season, and serving a punch will cut down considerably on the amount of time spent in mixing drinks. Moreover, a good punch recipe will amaze and impress your friends with very little effort on your part. (See the punch recipes in Chapter 5.) The amount you need depends on the strength of the punch; count on about four or five servings per person.

MIXERS

For every liter of light liquor that you have, you'll need about two quarts of mixers. The most common light-alcohol mixers are tonic water, fruit juice, and cola. Whiskey drinkers tend to add less to their liquor, so you can get away with buying less of dark-alcohol mixers, such as soda water, ginger ale, and light soft drinks (1 to 1½ quarts per liter). Estimate how much of each mixer you'll need and then buy a few extra liters of fruit juice and soft drinks in order to accommodate non-drinking guests. Also, make sure you have diet soda on hand if you're expecting weight-conscious guests.

ICE

Believe it or not, ice is probably the most important of all cocktail ingredients. If you run out of blended whiskey or gin, guests can at least switch to something else. There are no substitutes for ice, however, and just about anyone who's ever had a rum and Coke at room temperature will tell you it's unpleasant. For a typical four-hour party, plan on 1 lb. of ice per person. In winter, you could get away with only ¾ lbs., and in summer you should buy 1½ lbs. per guest. If you want to fill an ice chest for beer and wine, remember to get enough to fill the chest in addition to cocktail ice needs.

Check the Yellow Pages or ask at your liquor store; you may be able to find a local company from which you can order ice in quantity (by the 40 lb. bag, for example). Some places will deliver right to your home on the day of the party. Make sure to specify cocktail ice when you order so that you don't end up taking an ice pick to a 40 lb. bag (or, in frustration, any of your guests).

GARNISHES

For a basic bar, limes and lemons are essential, while orange slices are purely optional. Buy one lime for every four to six guests and cut the limes into wedges in advance. Cut lemons into twists and slices and cut oranges into slices; you'll need a supply of lemons and oranges to the tune of about one per 25 guests. Consider buying a jar of olives (a must for martinis), cocktail onions (optional—only if you're inviting a Gibson drinker), and cherries (for Manhattans). Fruit-cutting instructions and additional suggestions abound on pages 34-36.

FOOD

You shouldn't consider having a cocktail party of any size without offering some sort of food along with the drinks. At the very least, buy some peanuts, chips, or other snacks. Appetizers—cold vegetables and dip, cheese and crackers, or even more complicated hors d'oeuvres—are better. For more information, buy a cookbook.

UTENSILS

The basic bartending kit described in Chapter 2—available from Harvard Student Agencies—should take care of your utensil needs. Also make sure that you have at least one trash barrel, a large ice bucket, a sharp knife for cutting fruit, a water pitcher, a towel, and an ashtray for the bar. An ashtray may seem like a minor detail at this point, but if a line forms at the bar, any smokers in the group will invariably end up flicking burning embers wherever gravity takes them (a disaster if they land in the punch!).

NAPKINS

Remember to put out some cocktail napkins for your guests. For a nice touch, place the stack of napkins on the bar, put a shot glass in the center, and bear down firmly as you twist the glass clockwise. Remove the glass and you've created an attractive fanned design of cocktail napkins. Ooh-la-la!

GLASSWARE

Real glassware adds a touch of class to any party; on the other hand, broken glassware doesn't. You may want to opt for disposable plastic glasses, which are perfectly acceptable for even relatively high-brow gatherings. You need only two types: the lowball or on-the-rocks, which is short and wide and holds about 9 oz., and the highball, which is taller and holds 10 to 12 oz. Use the highball for popular highballs, beers, and Collinses, and the lowball for everything else—stirred cocktails, shaken drinks, on-the-rocks liquor, and wine. For a four-hour party, buy at least three per person, at a ratio of 75% highball to 25% lowball. For a dance party, plan on at least four per person; people tend to put the glasses down when they feel the Night Fever and then forget about them.

If you insist on real glasses, check the phone book for a general rental agency. Some will even deliver glasses to your home and pick them up again after the party.

▶ "HEY, NOT SO FAST! WHAT ABOUT SETTING UP FOR THE
PARTY? WHAT DO I DO THEN...?"

STEP 2: SETTING UP

Once you've gathered all your supplies together, you'll need to set them up in as efficient and attractive a manner as possible. The bar itself can be nothing more complicated than a table that's strong enough to support the weight of all the bottles and the occasional sideways lurch by a tipsy guest. Cover it with a plastic tablecloth for protection from spills and with a linen tablecloth over that if you're aiming for a classy appearance.

For small parties (fewer than 15 people), you don't need a bartender. A self-service bar, set up like the one in diagram 1, provides room for two guests to mix their own drinks. Parties of 20 to 100 people tend to run more smoothly with the help of a bartender. Diagrams 2 and 3 illustrate two possible setups for a one-person bar.

Large parties of over 100 guests require the services of at least two bartenders. In diagram 4, notice that the two bartenders share the mixers but have their own liquor bottles for speed and efficiency's sake.

Are you already tired of all this planning? Can't afford a big bash? Have a BYOB party instead—bring your own bottle. At a BYOB, each guest brings a contribution to the bar. It's impossible to diagram a BYOB setup (or outcome), so you'll just have to improvise.

Use common sense in setting up the party room. Avoid locating it near a doorway, where it will invariably block traffic. Try to put the bar against a wall; if you're tending bar yourself, set it up so that guests can't sneak around you and pour their own drinks. If this happens, your carefully planned, efficient layout will deteriorate rapidly, and in time your bar will be a mess. To avoid this fate, make an example of anyone who tries to cross into the bartender's territory by saying to them, "I would appreciate it if you stepped back."

STEP 3: WORKING THE PARTY

Once the party actually starts, your primary—and perhaps only—concern should be the maintenance of a smoothly running bar, making sure that it remains orderly and well stocked. The ease with which these tasks can be accomplished depends on the type of party you're having, but as long as you succeed in this challenge, all should be tickety-boo.

Unless guests are mixing their own drinks, keeping the bar orderly should be simple—just put all of the bottles and utensils back in their original place after you use them and you shouldn't have to do much more than pick up the occasional empty glass or wadded-up napkin. Take advantage of lulls in the action—whenever the bar clears out for a minute, take the time to tidy things up.

Keeping things supplied is a little more challenging. You'll invari-

Diagram 1: Self-Service Bar

Extra Mix

Napkins

Ashtray

Dry Vermouth

Sweet Vermouth

Scotch

Bourbon

Canadian

Triple Sec

Tequila

Rum

Gin

Vodka

Ashtray

Napkins

Extra Mix

Mix

Water

Towel

Garnishes

Glasses

Ice

Trash

Water

Towel

Mix

DIAGRAM 2: ONE - PERSON BAR

DIAGRAM 3: ONE-PERSON BAR

Diagram 4: Two-Person Bar

ably need to replace items like ice and mixers that may be as far away as the kitchen. This is complicated by a fundamental rule of bartending—never leave the bar unattended—and its corollary—if you leave it unattended, all hell will break lose and people will be jumping out the windows by the time you return. The rule holds true for nearly any gathering; even otherwise respectable, trustworthy adults will occasionally show the restraint of hyperactive, foaming-at-the-mouth children when left alone around a fully stocked bar.

So you've run out of ice and you're trapped behind the bar. What to do? Simply ask a friend, a co-worker, or anyone else who's available and won't mind helping to get another bag of ice. If you're in a situation where you don't know anyone at the party, look around for wallflowers (the folks who spend more time hovering around the peanut dish than talking to other guests). Every party usually has at least one, and he or she will probably welcome the sudden moment of attention before returning to the ignominy of loneliness.

It's a good idea to keep a snack—nothing more complicated than peanuts or pretzels is necessary—somewhere near the bar so that guests who are waiting for drinks will have something with which to occupy themselves.

For more details on how to look and act professional behind the bar, read Chapter 7. One professional prerequisite discussed there calls for some clarification here: tips. At a private party, a tip cup on the bar looks extremely tacky. On the other hand, if you work at a rather "impersonal" party, such as a large company gathering or some sort of dance, guests may appreciate the option of bribing you for faster or stronger drinks. In situations like this, ask the person who hired you if you may put out a tip cup. If you use one, put a dollar in at the beginning of the night to give guests a hint.

STEP 4: THROWING EVERYBODY OUT

This is actually much easier than it sounds. When you're ready to call it a night, simply start putting the bar away. First, pack up extra liquor and mixers and take them to the kitchen. Then take speedpourers out of the remaining bottles, put the caps on, and put those bottles away. Guests will quickly notice the absence of liquor; some will be annoyed, but most will eventually start heading home.

At this point, keep a careful eye out for guests who have had too much to drink. Never let an intoxicated guest drive home. This is not only extremely dangerous, but also legally actionable—party hosts can be sued for damages caused by drunken guests. If you find yourself in such a situation, either ask a sober guest to drive them home or call a cab.

PARTY CHECKLIST

Use this list—as well as the ordering summary that follows and your own common sense—as a guide when planning your party. Don't feel obligated to buy everything listed (unless your pockets are very deep); as always, tailor your purchases to the needs of your guests.

EQUIPMENT

shaker glass	corkscrew/bottle opener/can opener
shaker shell	ashtrays
jigger	bar napkins
speedpourers	water pitcher
bar spoon	dry and wet trash buckets
ice bucket	swizzle sticks/cocktail straws

LIQUOR

bourbon	tequila
blended whiskey	beer
Scotch	wine
vodka	dry vermouth
gin	sweet vermouth
rum	other liquors?

MIXERS

tonic water	Bloody Mary mix
cola	mixing juices
soda water	light cream
ginger ale	milk
Sprite or 7-Up	water
diet soda	Rose's lime juice
sour mix	

GLASSWARE (PLASTIC)

lowball	beer
highball	wine

GARBAGE/GARNISHES

lemon twists and slices	specialty garnishes (optional)
lime wedges	maraschino cherries (with stems)
orange slices	cocktail onions
olives (pitted and without pimentos)	

CONDIMENTS

bitters	Tabasco sauce
bar sugar	horseradish
nutmeg	Worcestershire
grenadine	pepper
salt	

(you might consider purchasing a pre-fabbed Bloody Mix at the liquor store in lieu of all these ingredients)

ORDERING SUMMARY

Liquor: 1 liter per 6 guests plus beer and wine
Mixer: 2 quarts per liter of light alcohol
1 quart per liter of dark alcohol
a selection for non-alcoholic drinks
Ice: ¾ lbs. per person in winter
1 lb. per person in moderate weather
1½ lbs. per person in summer
more as needed to fill wine and beer chests
Garnishes: 1 lime per 6 people (more in summer and for young people)
1 lemon per 25 people
1 orange per 25 people (optional)
Glasses: 3 per person (more for a dance party)
75% highball
25% lowball
Snacks: vary widely

PROFES-
SIONAL
BARTENDING

THIS IS IT—you've patiently learned every trick of the trade. You can set up a bar, throw a good cocktail party, mix any one of a hundred drinks in the blink of an eye, and even converse intelligently about the genealogy of gin. And now, you want what every good American wants—a paycheck.

And why not? Whether you're looking for part-time work or a full-fledged career, bartending can be both a fun and an interesting job. Furthermore, you can make a pretty good living at it in some of the choicer bars. In the first half of this chapter, we'll tell you how to find a job—where and how to look for a place that fits your talents. In the second half, we'll tell you how to act on the job—what to wear, what to do, and what not to do as a professional bartender.

ONE: "SIR, I THINK I'M GOING TO HAVE TO CUT YOU OFF!"
TWO: "HEY, I DON'T HAVE TO TAKE THIS KIND OF ABUSE FROM AN 18TH CENTURY PIRATE!"

LOOKING FOR A JOB

High employee turnover makes bartending an ideal job to break into. If you hit the right place at the right time, presto—well...okay, it's not quite that easy. Remember how we explained each drink-mixing process as though a two-year-old child could get it? When you start dealing with professionals in real bars, it's not quite that simple. Working in a high-class bar requires speed and efficiency, and the only way you can develop these skills in through experience. No matter how many times you carefully read Chapter 2 or how many drink recipes you diligently memorized in Chapter 3, you will not be able to stroll into the Ritz tomorrow and land a job. Chances are, you'll have to start near the bottom of the proverbial totem pole before working your way up.

The good news here is that the bottom of the bartending world isn't necessarily the worst place in the world. You don't have to start out in a miserable spot where the boss is an ape and the customers are baboons. Rather, "bottom" generally refers to places where you won't make much money—the low salaries, poor customers, and empty bar rooms won't pay your rent. Compensation for hard work at the bottom comes in the form of the speed, efficiency, and experience that you will gain so that you can move up to the next, higher-paying tier.

There are a number of different types of businesses that hire bartenders. They are listed below in roughly ascending order according to the amount of experience you need to get hired. Keep in mind, however, that this will vary considerably according to the individual business. Extremely posh catering services, for example, will probably be more selective than those that cater to Little League banquets. Of course, most Little League banquets won't require a bartender anyway...unless it's an event from one of those nefarious national teams that fudges the ages of its players.

1. CATERING OR TEMPORARY SERVICES

Bartending at catered events is usually an undemanding experience, and most caterers are willing to hire people with little or no experience. Unfortunately, tips (if allowed) are not very large at catered events, and you probably won't make a lot of money at these jobs. The best way to find a caterer in your area is to check the Yellow Pages.

2. HOTELS WITH BANQUET FACILITIES

These are very similar to catering jobs; most are low pressure and low paying. Frequently, hotels will have an office for hiring staff of all varieties, making it the right place to inquire about available jobs.

3. HARBOR CRUISES

This option is obviously limited to people who live near large bodies of water. Also known as "booze cruises," these jobs are usually a little more demanding than catering work (not least because some people find the combination of seasickness and liquor to be unsettling). Most of the companies that offer these cruises have offices directly on the docks. Tips will vary widely depending upon who rents the boat.

4. AIRPORT/TRAIN STATION BARS

These are also low-pressure jobs. Unfortunately, tips are usually terrible. Many times these bars are owned by outside corporations that pay rent to the airport/station in exchange for space, so a manager might be harder to track down in person. Be persistent; jobs in these venues are easier to come by than you might think.

5. HOTEL AND RESTAURANT BARS

These vary widely depending on the quality of the hotel or restaurant. In larger restaurants, you can find work at the service bar, where you'll make drinks to be served by the waiters and waitresses. These provide good experience, but since you won't be in contact with the customers, you will frequently not get tips (although some establishments will include service bartenders in the pooled tips collection).

6. LOCAL BARS WITHOUT LARGE CROWDS

These are your typical neighborhood bars—cozy, friendly, and usually very quiet (think about what Cheers looked like most of the time). If there's a strong contingent of "regulars" (Norm and Cliff excepted), you can make decent tips. However, the less crowded the bar, the fewer tips you'll get.

7. PUBLIC BARS

These are the large-capacity, crowded bars and nightclubs where customers stand two or three deep at the bar on the weekends and the bartenders are usually run ragged until closing time. These are the highest-paying jobs, but they're also the most demanding. Don't expect to land one of these jobs without experience.

Perhaps you are asking yourself, "How do I get a job at one of these here places?" One of the first things you'll have to do is to stop talking to yourself—bars don't like to hire folks whom they perceive as crazy. There's no single method that's guarantees success; however, there are a few different approaches that you can take.

OVERHEARD:

"...SO, I TELL YOU, I WAS WORKING AT THIS PLACE IN THE HAMPTONS, REAL FANCY KIND OF PLACE—LOTS OF MIRRORS, LOTS OF BRASS, AND THIS FAUX NAUTICAL THEME THAT WAS ACTUALLY DONE IN A PRETTY TASTEFUL WAY—WHICH IS REALLY SURPRISING FOR NAUTICAL THEMES, SO OFTEN FALLING TO HACKNEYED TROPES THAT YOU ONLY GET FROM INTERIOR DESIGNERS WHO HAVE PROBABLY NEVER SEEN THE SEA OR FROM OVER-EARNEST SMALL BUSINESS OWNERS WHO ARE BLINDED TO THEIR OWN OUTRIGHT AWFULNESS BY THE SAME KIND OF QUASI-FAMILIAL LOVE THAT LETS PARENTS HANG THEIR CHILDREN'S WORK ON EVERY AVAILABLE BIT OF WALL SPACE, EVEN (AND ALMOST ESPECIALLY) IF IT'S COMPLETELY WITHOUT ANY KIND OF MERIT, ARTISTIC OR OTHERWISE...OH, SO YEAH...YEAH...I GOT A MILLION STORIES LIKE THAT...WHAT?...OH...OH, I GUESS ONE TIME I SERVED THIS GUY WHO HAD, I THINK, SIX FINGERS...I THINK."

APPLY DIRECTLY TO THE MANAGER

Find a place that looks appealing, stroll right in, and ask to see the manager. If they're not currently hiring, they might be soon; leave a resume or make sure that the manager knows how to contact you if an opening emerges. Never look for work during peak hours, since both the manager and the rest of the employees will probably be busy preparing and will resent you for interrupting them. The best time to approach a bar looking for work is between 2 and 4 p.m., when the manager should be around while not overwhelmed with work. Never ask another bartender if that particular place is hiring; they will almost always say no, regardless of the truth in the matter, since bartenders often have other bartending friends (presumably not you) who they would like to see hired.

USE PERSONAL CONNECTIONS

As in any job hunt, this should not be underestimated. If you happen to be the friend of a bartender, you've got a leg up on anyone else who is applying. An acquaintance with a current employee who can pro-vide you with a good recommendation is a definite advantage.

BE WILLING NOT TO START AS A BARTENDER

There are essentially two bar jobs other than bartending—working the door and working as a barback. If you're hired by a bar and you don't have much experience, chances are you'll be asked to start at one of these jobs and work your way up to tending bar in a couple of months. Beware of bait-and-switch tactics on the part of the manager—if it becomes clear that he or she has no intention of promoting you, it might be a good idea to start looking for another job.

Working the door is essentially a dead-end job. You'll be able to pick up a fair amount of knowledge about how a bar is run, but you won't get any hands-on experience. Working as a barback, on the other hand, is a much better way to learn the bartending trade. A barback, also known as a "bar rat" in seedy and less-flattering environs, is essentially a bartending apprentice. Your responsibilities would include tapping kegs, running ice, replacing glassware, stocking garnishes, and so on. You'll have the opportunity to observe closely the bartenders who you're backing up, so keep your eyes open, file away any questions that come to mind, and query the bartenders whenever there's a lull. If you develop a good relationship with your bartenders (in the professional sense, of course), you may be asked to set up drinks (that is, put everything in the drink except the alcohol). After a few weeks of this type of experience, you should be ready to make the move to bartending.

OFFER TO TAKE A SLOW SHIFT

You may not have a choice in this matter. Slow shifts such as lunch bar shifts, Sunday brunches, and possibly Monday or Tuesday nights offer the same pluses and minuses as working in an uncrowded bar; you'll be under less pressure to perform, although your tips won't be as substantial.

DON'T LIE ABOUT YOUR EXPERIENCE

Outright lying or merely exaggerating about your experience might get you a job, but it's a poor idea. Bartending is a learned craft, and if you lie your way into a job that's beyond your experience level, you'll be found out after an hour and quite possibly thrown out on your ear. Lying is also wrong and [somewhat dated presidential joke deleted — eds.].

LOOK FOR SEASONAL WORK

Summer and winter tourist spots usually hire many more employees during the high season. The advantages are obvious—not only there more job opportunities and more customers (meaning bigger tips), but you'll also probably be working near either a beach or a ski slope. If you want to find this sort of summer work, start looking far in advance. For example, if you want a summer job on Cape Cod, start your search when there's still snow on the ground and all the other would-be bartenders are still skiing. Cruise ships also offer interesting bartending opportunities as long as you're prepared for a major lifestyle change. Most hire out of Miami and New York.

FIND OUT IF A LOCAL UNION HAS A REFERRAL SERVICE

In some cities, the local Hotel and Restaurant, Institutional Employees, and Bartenders Union offers a job referral service to its members. Large hotels, restaurant chains, and other unionized establishments sometimes hire directly through the union, so membership will spare you the tedious door-knocking that might otherwise be necessary. Call your local union to inquire; if it doesn't have a referral service, don't bother to join—there's no point in paying union dues when you're unemployed.

CULTIVATE CURRENT EMPLOYERS AS REFERENCES

Never consciously alienate an employer, regardless of his or her ogre-like leanings. When you're looking for that prestigious second (or third or fourth) job, your potential future employer will want to know how well you performed in your previous position. Be prepared to provide names and phone numbers of former employers as references. If you really did annoy your last boss, it's probably not a good idea to list him or her as a reference.

DON'T GET DISCOURAGED

inding a first job can be tedious and frustrating. Above all, don't get discouraged. Be persistent and patient. Speak as politely in your 40th interview as you did in your first. Emphasize how hard you'll work and your willingness to accept low pay in exchange for experience.

ACTING LIKE A PROFESSIONAL

APPEARANCE

Bartending is a service profession, which means that only half the job involves making drinks well and efficiently. The other half requires that you make people happy—a bartender has to learn how to please both the customer and the managers at the same time.

A clean, spiffy appearance is crucial for professional bartending. In a restaurant, the manager can hide a grubby, slovenly, vermin-infested cook back in the kitchen if need be. By contrast, bartenders work right up front, handling ice and fruit in full view of the customers. Obviously, a good bartender must look immaculate and well groomed; drinks prepared by a sloppy bartender with dirty hands are rather unappealing.

Most bar managers will tell you what to wear when they hire you; most will request that you wear clothes appropriate to the bar's style. Whatever you wear, always look neat and comfortable so that you can maintain a cool, confident bartending demeanor, even after several hectic hours. If you're allowed to choose your dress in a somewhat fancy place or a catering agency, or if you're self-employed, stick with traditional bar attire. Men wear dark pants and shoes with a white shirt and a bow tie. The bow tie idea might sound silly, but long ties have an irritating tendency to fall into the drinks that you mix. A bow tie might make you look like Pee Wee Herman, but it will provide essential freedom of movement. Women should wear a dark skirt or slacks with a white blouse. Long-haired representatives of both sexes should tie their tresses back neatly.

Try to keep your appearance behind the bar as close to neutral as possible. A good bartender is like a good vodka—he or she promotes a pleasant feeling of well-being, but blends easily into many surroundings. Both men and women should avoid wearing flashy jewelry, political buttons, and outrageous clothing; if you have any doubts regarding the neutrality of a hair style or article of clothing, do not sport it. Some bars may promote a hipper, more colorful image, but most prefer the conservative look. Use your own judgment in these matters, but remember that, while your customers probably won't speak up and tell you when your appearance has offended them, they'll pass along a little message in their tips (or lack thereof).

ATTITUDE

In a way, this aspect of bartending is more important than anything else. Mix a screwdriver with the wrong amount of vodka and nobody will notice. Annoy a customer and the whole bar will hear about it.

Whatever happens, look like you know what you're doing. Nine times out of ten, a confident attitude will fool the customer, even if you have no idea what goes in a rum and Coke. If you maintain the image of authority, patrons won't question your ability to mix a drink or your decision to shut off a drunk. Customers and bar managers get uncomfortable when they see their bartender stumbling around and looking noticeably confused, or if they see a scowling, irritable, mumbling bar keep. Always smile (or at least look cocky), grab bottles by the neck surely and swiftly, speak clearly and positively, and act like you know every drink ever invented.

That last word of wisdom needs a bit of clarification. Don't feel mortified if you must ask the customer what goes into a drink. You should feel properly stupid if you don't know how to make a gin and tonic, but nobody expects you to remember what goes into a Pink Squirrel. Don't be afraid to ask, and don't rule out the possibility of bluffing a bit since the customer probably doesn't even know the ingredients of the really exotic drinks. Why embarrass him or her by asking?

If you do completely screw up a drink, you can usually talk your way out of it. One former instructor of the Harvard Bartending Course used to tell the following tale: once, when he was just beginning his illustrious career, a customer ordered a Hop-Skip-and-Go-Naked. The instructor vaguely remembered that the drink must be pretty strong to merit such a name, so he confidently sauntered to the back bar, threw in a little of this, a dash of that, a few ounces of flavored brandies, some coloring, several rums, and three garnishes. He presented the masterpiece with a flourish to the customer, who stared at the concoction in horror and protested, "But that's not 1 oz. vodka, 1 oz. gin, and the juice from half a lime, filled with beer!" Without missing a beat, the instructor replied, "Oh! You wanted a Western Hop-Skip-and-Go-Naked! I made you the Eastern version!"

Don't forget that line—you might need it some day. Many drinks vary drastically between regions of the country, bars, or recipe books.

Just try to keep on top of the variations as much as possible, and act confident even when you're not.

COURTESY

THE CUSTOMER IS ALWAYS RIGHT (EVEN IF STUPID)

However painful it may be to follow this axiom in practice, the customer is always right. If a patron accuses you of making a drink improperly, at least go through the motions of altering it according to his or her wishes. Sometimes a difficult customer has had a hard day, just wants a little more attention, or happens to be a complete jerk. Never say, "No, you're wrong. The recipe for a White Russian does not call for mayonnaise." Nobody ever got rich by taking the moral high ground.

Always treat customers courteously; never hurry them or show irritation. The moment a customer arrives, you should spring into action: smile, greet the guest warmly, and drop whatever you were doing to wait on him or her. Try to remember the faces (names, if introduced) and tastes of your regular customers so that you can ask them if they want "the usual" as soon as they come in. This is very clichéd, but it also happens to be appreciated in the extreme by customers. Once someone has established the rapport of a regular, tips invariably increase.

Be aware of whom you talk to and when. Never appear to be listening in on a conversation or trying to take part. As soon as you have served a drink, step back from the customer or move away. Some folks will want to talk to you...desperately. You'll quickly learn to spot those people, and if you bartend long enough, you'll probably devise ingenious ways in which to avoid long conversations about their personal problems. On the other hand, a couple having a personal argument doesn't want to hear your opinion on the matter, so give them a wide berth. If invited to chat with someone for a moment, never talk about another customer or gossip about scandals you've witnessed at the bar (including your own—it's safer and more professional to leave your personal life at home).

If you must answer a telephone at the bar, do so quietly. If the call is for a patron, never say that the person is there. Instead offer to inquire, and leave it up to the customer to decide whether to answer the phone.

Customers who smoke should be indulged regardless of the medical consequences. If a customer reaches for a cigarette, light it. Replace ashtrays regularly and correctly, placing a clean ashtray over the dirty one and lifting both from the bar (to avoid scattering ashes all over the place), then place the clean tray on the table. Of course, some states and cities are now passing ordinances to prohibit smoking in bars, in which case, definitely do not light your customers cigarette. You can commiserate with a crest-fallen smoker, decrying the jack-booted thuggery of such ordinances (although keep in mind that these laws are intended to protect bar workers from second-hand smoke), but enforce the laws on this issue.

Ultimately, you should do everything in your power to make sure that your customers are happy. Learn which customers—both as individuals and, if you work in a bar without established regulars, as stereotypes—like to be pampered and which like to be left more or less alone when their glass is not empty. The bottom line is tips: your aim is to maximize the tips you make, and the happier the customer, the larger the tip.

DEFERENCE

YES, BOSS. RIGHT AWAY, MA'AM. ANYTHING YOU SAY, SIR.

Bartenders who offend customers just lose their tips. Bartenders who offend the boss lose their jobs. Of course, one way to offend the boss is to offend the customers—but if the customer is always right, the boss is always just a little bit more right. Managers expect all bartenders, even beginners, to adhere to a set of commonsense guidelines. Therefore, if you want to keep your job, get raises, work better shifts, and earn a flattering job reference, you'd best impress the boss.

Managers and customers think highly of a busy, hard-working bartender. Even during a lull period, you can always find plenty to do around the bar: wipe spills, wash glasses, clean ashtrays, cut fruit, make pre-mixes (such as sour mix or Bloody Mary mix), and pick up dirty glasses, straws, and napkins. Even when you talk to customers, look busy and you'll make a good impression on everybody.

Even if you don't hit that lull period, take a few seconds here and there to keep the bar clean. Customers won't want to drink at a messy, littered bar, so managers always frown upon a slob behind the bar.

If you're looking for the quickest, easiest way to get fired, try cheating on your boss. Bar managers have usually worked in the business for a long time and can tell when a bartender takes a few dollars here and there or serves free drinks to friends. In fact, managers even notice when a bartender has a heavy hand with liquor bottles. If inventories fall especially low after a certain bartender's shift, that person has poured too much into each drink. Be stingy (within reason). Also, be thrifty regarding which brands you use. In most operations, you'll be told to put the cheapest ("house" brands) in a drink unless the customer requests a "call" or a "premium" brand (for a refresher on these terms, review Basic Bar Setup, page 10-11).

If you want to get canned really fast, have a few drinks. Drinking on the job makes you an inefficient bartender and proves that you have no respect for the bar or the customers. All you have to do is to spill a drink, slur a few words, or insult a customer—before you can even hiccup, you'll be on the unemployment lines faster than George Costanza.

As you shower your boss with attention, don't ignore co-workers. Treat them with courtesy, too. Make sure to leave the bar clean, orderly, and well stocked with supplies at the end of your shift. If someone asks you to fill in for a shift, do so whenever possible. Of course, co-workers can't fire you for an unpleasant disposition, but bar work is much more fun when employees get along well and help each other.

MONEY

PASSING THE BUCKS

Proficiency in handling money requires practice. In busy bars, many errors result from giving change for the wrong amount of money, such as when a bartender mistakes a ten-dollar bill for a twenty (harder to do now that the bloated, titanic head of Andrew Jackson stares down his handlers). To minimize these errors, follow the process of the "five C's": collect cash; call it; cash register; correct till-slot; and count change back.

1. COLLECT CASH

So you don't forget in the confusion of a busy bar, collect the money for a drink right after you serve it. If your bar has a tab or check system, the manager will teach you the correct procedure to follow.

2. CALL IT

"Call" the amount of money. When the customer hands you the bill, say, "That's two-fifty out of ten." You'll be more likely to remember exactly what you have after audibly stating it.

3. CASH REGISTER

Keep the bill on top of the cash register until you hand the customer the change. You will remember the bill that you received, and will be protected if the customer insists, "But I gave you a 20, not a 10."

4. CORRECT TILL-SLOT

Get in the habit of putting each denomination in the correct till-slot of the cash register. Then, if the customer says that you incorrectly counted the change, check the register to see if you put the bill in the wrong slot.

5. COUNT CHANGE BACK

Count the change back to the customer, saying, "Two-fifty out of ten: here's fifty cents for three dollars, two more to make five, and five more makes ten," as you hand back the money.

If you cannot satisfactorily handle a customer complaint, call the manager. Usually, money complications become the manager's responsibility. Don't be insulted, however, if the manager returns the customer's money without question—remember that the customer is always right. If a similar problem occurs involving the same customer a second time, you and the manager should proceed cautiously. You're probably getting suckered.

You will also have to handle tip money in a bar. Some places pool all the tips earned in a given shift and then split the money equally among all the bartenders. This method is equitable when bartenders share areas and, therefore, customers. Never announce the amount of a tip, no matter how great or small. It's embarrassing to the customer. Not only that, it's very tacky.

DUTY

FEARLESSNESS IS FOR SUCKAS

Protect yourself and your employer. Read the section in Chapter 6 on the bartender's responsibility carefully. Given the evolution of judicial attitudes toward liability, bartenders and managers are forced to assume more responsibility for the people who they serve these days. If you do your job correctly, you will probably have to cut off a drunk from time to time. This is not much fun, but it is considerably more fun than losing a liquor license, paying a massive fine, or doing time in the Big House.

SHE: "WHEN ARE YOU GOING OUT TO GET THAT BARTENDING JOB YOU PROMISED YOU'D GET TWO MONTHS AGO!"
HE: "BABY, COOL OUT, THIS IS ONLY CHAPTER 7!"

8

SIDE EFFECTS & CONSEQUENCES

SIDE EFFECTS & CONSEQUENCES

LIKE MOST OTHER pastimes and indulgences, alcohol is best enjoyed in moderation. A glass or two of wine with dinner, hot buttered rum by the fireplace on a cold winter day, a hot dog and a beer at the ballpark—scenes like these are so idyllic that they make the pernicious world of alcohol advertisements seem almost believable. Taken at the right time and in reasonable amounts, alcohol can genuinely enhance your life.

Unfortunately, alcohol can also ruin your life. Some of the damage that alcohol wreaks on the careless and stupid is minor enough to be almost amusing. Remember the worst hangover of your life? Most people do, in vivid, graphic, horrifying detail. The average college student, for example, knows more synonyms for vomiting than does the average Eskimo for snow. A "beer gut" can also be good for a laugh, especially when it belongs to someone else.

Other alcohol-related problems, however, are less easy to joke about. An overdose of alcohol can be fatal even to the healthiest person. Alcoholism—once considered the province of bums and winos—is now universally recognized as a disease that can strike people from any social or economic group. Finally, drunk drivers account for nearly half of all American traffic fatalities, and many of the victims of these accidents are innocent motorists who just happened to be in the wrong place at the wrong time.

Alcohol is a drug that can be both used and abused. Whether you plan to serve it or just drink it, you should be aware of its side effects. In this chapter, we'll discuss:

THE PHYSIOLOGY OF ALCOHOL

How the body metabolizes alcohol. How a person becomes drunk. How much an individual can drink before being considered drunk.

HANGOVERS

The causes of hangovers. Modern science's unsuccessful quest for a cure.

OTHER SIDE EFFECTS

Liquor's effect on other parts of the body besides the brain. The direct link between alcohol and unsightly weight problems.

SERIOUS SIDE EFFECTS

Alcohol abuse and the problem drinker. Drinking and driving.

BARTENDERS' AND HOSTS' RESPONSIBILITIES

Legal issues.

PHYSIOLOGY

BRAIN DRAIN

Always do sober what you said you'd do drunk. That will teach you to keep your mouth shut.
—Ernest Hemingway

Your body actually produces small amounts of alcohol naturally, transforming food sugars into about 1 oz. of ethanol each day (hence the phrase "high on life..."). When it takes in additional alcohol, however, the excess is absorbed into the bloodstream and affects various parts of the body until the alcohol eventually oxidizes.

Liquor contains ethyl alcohol. The primary distinction between ethyl and other alcohols is that ethanol metabolizes rapidly into relatively harmless substances, whereas the other alcohols metabolize slowly into poisons. It is extremely unwise to drink any type of alcohol other than ethyl. Even a small amount of isopropyl (rubbing) alcohol can cause permanent blindness, and a larger amount can be fatal.

Three basic steps take place when the body processes alcohol: absorption, distribution, and oxidation. In the absorption phase, alcohol—unlike most foods—passes rapidly into the bloodstream without being digested. Certain variables alter this process. Have you ever noticed that you get drunk faster on an empty stomach? Food keeps

QUIZ:

Q: WHAT IS WRONG WITH THIS DIAGRAM?

alcohol in the stomach longer (where absorption takes place rapidly). Bear in mind, however, that the alcohol will eventually make it to the small intestine, so gorging yourself will only delay the effects. Does champagne make you feel tipsy faster than wine? Bubbles make you get drunk faster. The carbon dioxide in any carbonated drink hastens the movement of alcohol through the stomach to the small intestine and into the bloodstream.

Body weight is also a major consideration in the attempt to gauge alcohol's effect on the drinker. Since the bloodstream distributes alcohol uniformly throughout the body, larger people—whose bloodstreams cover a lot more ground—will feel the effect of a given number of drinks less strongly than smaller people.

Once the alcohol enters the bloodstream, it passes to body organs in proportion to the amount of water they contain. The most immediate and noticeable characteristics of drunkenness occur as a result of alcohol's effect on the brain, which contains a high concentration of water. The most pronounced brain responses vary directly with the amount of alcohol measured in the bloodstream. For that reason, a fairly good indication of intoxication is a measurement called the blood alcohol concentration (BAC), the percentage of alcohol in the bloodstream. (Sometimes this measurement is referred to as the BAL—the blood alcohol level.) Alcohol is a depressant, so when the BAC rises, more areas of the brain become depressed. Reactions to alcohol vary tremendously among individuals, but when the BAC reaches 0.05% in the average person, the outer layer of the brain becomes drugged and sluggish. This outer layer controls inhibitions, self-restraint, and judgment—or rather, it did when it was sober. When alcohol numbs this control center, most inhibitions fly out the proverbial window, and drinkers usually find that they have a lot more to say about everything. Given this new-found sociability and vivaciousness, people often forget that alcohol is a depressant (a frequently heard croon from the mouths of the tipsy: "How could I be so happy if it's a depressant?"). After all, any drug that leads you to call your boss a clown to his face while belching loudly enough to win a contest at the county fair must be a stimulant. Remember, however, that this feeling stems from the depression of a brain part, not the stimulation of it.

At a BAC of 0.10%, the motor area of the brain (anterior) becomes depressed and coordination becomes quite impaired. The drinker staggers, slurs words, and can't quite fit the key in the keyhole. By this point, just about all inhibitions have been drowned.

At 0.20% BAC, alcohol affects the mid-brain, the section that controls emotional behavior. At this stage, it is next to impossible for the drinker to appear sober. Sensory and motor skills have deteriorated to the point where many drinkers need to lie down. Some laugh, some cry, some become angry, some feel romantic...and some feel all these emotions at the same time, resulting in abject confusion.

A 0.30% BAC depresses the lower portion of the brain, which controls sensory perception. At this level, drinkers virtually lose consciousness; although awake, they have very little comprehension of the world around them. As the saying goes, "The lights are on, but no one's home." This is the point at which many drinkers "black out"—after sobering up, they will have no memory of their actions. Considering the way most people with a 0.30% act, this can be a mixed blessing.

Between 0.35% and 0.45% BAC, the party's over. A drinker at this level enters a coma and should be brought to a hospital. A BAC of 0.35% is generally the minimum level that causes death, so a coma is the body's defense mechanism against death. In this state, a patient will not drink anymore, so the body stands a better chance of keeping its BAC down to a survivable level.

At 0.60% BAC, the part of the brain that controls those little everyday activities, like breathing and heartbeat, becomes depressed. At this point, fatality is usually inevitable. A 0.60% BAC is actually easier to reach than you might think—chugging a fifth of liquor, for example, will probably kill you in 10 minutes (Nicolas Cage's character in Leaving Las Vegas excepted—to reiterate: Hollywood does not depict reality).

The following list summarizes the effects of the blood alcohol concentration (BAC) on the brain of an average person. These responses vary, however, from person to person and from day to day—see below for an explanation of other factors that affect intoxication. The second list approximates the number of drinks it takes the average person to reach these levels.

BAC (%)	EFFECTS
.05	Release of inhibitions and self-restraint; poor judgment
.10	Loss of coordination—staggering, slurring, clumsiness, impaired vision
.20	Dulled sensory perception; loss of emotional control
.30	Virtual loss of consciousness; blackout
.35-.45	Coma; minimum lethal level
.60	Death

OTHER FACTORS

Weight/alcohol consumption data such as that shown here provides a handy drinking formula that allows you to figure out how drunk you will be after each drink. Do not rely on these charts, however. The only variables that they take into consideration are weight, time, number of drinks consumed, and sometimes gender (to account for different metabolisms). In reality, many other factors play an important role in determining degrees of intoxication.

SLEEP
How much sleep did the drinker get last night? A tired person will show the effects of alcohol more readily than an alert drinker.

OTHER DRUGS
Did the drinker take any medication? Medicine alters alcohol's effects, sometimes drastically. Be very cautious mixing any two drugs, especially when one of them is alcohol.

AGE
Younger people usually become drunk on fewer drinks. Among older drinkers, vision deteriorates more rapidly as the BAC increases.

MOOD
Is the drinker in a good mood? An especially happy, sad, angry, or other mood probably will alter the person's response to alcohol.

METABOLISM
How does the drinker's metabolism work? Some people oxidize alcohol faster than others. As a result, BAC can vary widely even when many other factors remain constant.

FOOD
Drinking on an empty stomach accelerates the rate of alcohol absorption into the bloodstream. On an empty stomach, the bloodstream can absorb alcohol in as little as two to three minutes.

POTENCY
The strength of the beverage can obviously speed up or stave off intoxication. If drinks are being made with more than the standard amount of liquor, the drinker will get drunk faster.

LIVER FUNCTION
The organ, not the food. (Sorry, that was awful...) A healthy liver plays a major role in the sobering process and thus greatly influences the degree of inebriation.

RELATIONSHIPS AMONG SEX, WEIGHT, ORAL ALCOHOL
CONSUMPTION, AND BLOOD ALCOHOL LEVEL

BLOOD ALCOHOL LEVELS
(mg/100 mL)

ALCOHOL (OZ.)	DRINKS* PER HR.	FEMALE 100 LBS.	FEMALE 150 LBS.	MALE 150 LBS.	MALE 200 LBS.
½	1	.045	.03	.025	.019
1	2	.09	.06	.05	.037
2	4	.18	.12	.10	.07
3	6	.27	.18	.15	.11
4	8	.36	.24	.20	.15
5	10	.45	.30	.25	.18

One drink contains 1 oz. of 100-proof spirits, a 12 oz. beer, a 5 oz. wine, or a 3 oz. sherry.
SOURCE: Ray, Oakley: Drugs, Society, and Human Behavior, 3d ed. (St. Louis: C.V. Mosby
Co., 1983). Used by permission.

*One faulty assumption people often make is that beer or wine will not
get them as drunk as a drink with higher-proof liquor. Wrong. A cocktail, a beer, a 5 oz. glass of wine, and a 3 oz. glass of sherry all have
about the same amount of pure alcohol in them (0.6 oz.).*

SOBERING UP

Although alcohol moves quickly into the body and takes rapid effect,
getting it out of the system takes a long time. Sobering up occurs
through a process called oxidation, in which the liver breaks alcohol
down into water and carbon dioxide. In the case of most foods, the
rate of oxidation increases with activity. That is, as the body needs
more energy, it breaks down the food faster. Alcohol, however, has a
constant rate of oxidation that cannot be increased through exercise
(making it a worthless technique when trying to sober up). For most
people, that rate is about 0.5 oz. of alcohol (about one drink) per
hour.

In other words sobering up is simply a matter of time. All the black
coffee, brisk walks, fresh air, and cold showers in the world will not
speed it up. In fact, coffee can worsen things, as it can prove volatile
for a rather sensitive stomach, and the last thing that you need when
you're in a drunken stupor is to be in an energetic, confused stupor.

THE HANGOVER

Headache. Nausea. Stomach pains. An almost indescribable thirst. And—good lord! Who's that person on the other side of the bed??!

Hangovers can be remarkably debilitating. Drink a pint or two of tequila and chances are high that you won't spend more than half of the next day out of bed. Unless, of course, you have to go to work, in which case you'll spend more than half the day wishing that you were still in bed. While hangovers vary widely depending on a number of factors, too much of any kind of alcohol will inevitably give you one.

Most of the agony you feel when you're hungover is caused by dehydration. Remember the 13 trips you took to the bathroom during last night's blowout? When the body processes alcohol, it uses up large amounts of water; this will not only make you very thirsty in the morning but will also produce a headache and an overall feeling of sluggishness.

The variety of additives and spices added to liquor during production and mixing comprise the second major hangover culprit. Your nausea and stomach pains can be attributed in part to a number of flavoring herbs and spices in the liquor itself; as a general rule, cheaper liquor is more likely to contain impurities and hangover-inducing, stomach-churning additives, and liqueurs are more likely than other spirits to contain herbs and spices that will upset your stomach. Certain mixers can also lead to trouble—for example, the citric acid contained in the orange juice of an evening's worth of screwdrivers will probably not do your digestive system any favors (unless you consider nausea to be a gift rising up toward the heavens).

Unfortunately, there is no reliable "cure" for a hangover, despite what your Uncle Krazy Karl might be screaming from the attic. Only time—and, if possible, a long afternoon nap—will heal your self-inflicted wounds. There are, however, a few things you can do to minimize the pain.

First, drink plenty of water before bed. Drink until you're full and then drink some more. Keep a pitcher of water beside your bed in case you wake up during the night so that you can drink more. Depending on your level of drunkenness, this should counteract a great deal of the dehydration that causes hangovers. If you fell asleep before drinking water the night before, drink plenty the next morning. Resist the temptation to drink orange juice, as the acid contained therein might exacerbate your stomach pains.

Second, take a shower, sauna, or steam bath in the morning (not too long in the sauna or steam bath). Any of these will increase circulation and refresh and open pores, which should make you feel and look a bit less like death.

Third, take a non-aspirin pain reliever. You should avoid aspirin, which may upset your stomach. A couple of these pain relievers, especially after drinking a lot of water the night before, should reduce headache pain and other general body aches.

Even if you're really drunk and can't face the possibility of a massive hangover, avoid the temptation to empty your stomach. Although vomiting will prevent most of the alcohol left in your stomach from passing into the bloodstream and will rid your stomach of all those irritating additives, spices, and mixers, the harmful physiological side effects of induced vomiting far outweigh even the worst of hangovers. If the body decides to "clean house," you won't need to make yourself sick.

An old proverb recommends taking "a hair of the dog that bit you" (drinking more) in order to cure a hangover—logic that seems about as reasonable as the erstwhile Scottish belief that applying a few hairs of the canine that bit you would cure a wound. The person who came up with this phrase is probably long since dead; the idea certainly deserves its demise. Drinking a small amount of alcohol on a hangover will probably postpone but not eliminate the damage, but taking a restorative morning drink is a habit that's very likely to lead to alcoholism. Further, you will make your liver most unhappy if, while it's trying to rid itself of all that leftover booze, you ingest more. The dog will bite again.

OTHER SIDE EFFECTS

FAT

If you're weight conscious, alcohol is the worst of both worlds—it has absolutely no nutritional value, yet it contains a large number of calories. Even worse, the mixers that you usually ingest along with most liquors tend to be very fattening as well. The calorie counts may vary depending upon the recipe, but if you're watching your weight and would like a drink, try a light beer, a glass of wine, a wine spritzer or cooler, or perhaps the pineapple-wine cooler listed on page 95. If you prefer a distilled spirit, drink it either without the mixer, with soda water, or with a low-calorie mixer. Take a look at the following charts:

ALCOHOLIC BEVERAGE	AMOUNT	CALORIES
Beer, ale	12 oz.	about 150
Light beer	12 oz.	about 95
Distilled liquors		
80 proof	1½ oz.	97
86 proof	1½ oz.	105
94 proof	1½ oz.	116
Dry table wine	4 oz.	75-100

MIXERS	AMOUNT	CALORIES
Soda water	any	0
Cola	8 oz.	96
Ginger ale	8 oz.	72
Tonic water	8 oz.	72
Sour mix	4 oz.	about 50
Orange juice	8 oz	100
Cranberry juice	8 oz.	145

FATTY DRINKS	AMOUNT	CALORIES
Margarita	12 oz.	375
Piña Colada	12 oz.	350
Sangría	12 oz.	250
Frozen Daiquiri	12 oz.	300
Strawberry Daiquiri	12 oz.	350
Tom Collins	12 oz.	225

SHORT TERM

The brain isn't the only part of your body to notice the presence of alcohol. Even just one drink causes some rather harmless changes in the body; more liquor provokes more serious reactions.

The first drink or two affects the digestive system. It stimulates gastric juices in the stomach and possibly provokes a reaction in the taste buds, both of which serve to increase appetite. For this reason, people often enjoy apéritifs before meals. Apéritifs, alcoholic beverages drunk before the meal to stimulate the appetite, should be rather low in alcohol and not too warm or cold. A glass of wine, a beer, or a cocktail fits this description and serves as a good apéritif.

Too much alcohol might have the opposite effect it will stop diges-tion and probably deaden taste buds, thus reducing appetite. On the other hand, some people eat every potato chip in sight whenever they drink too much. (It was these people—and the malicious Brits—who caused the Irish Potato Famine.) This is due more properly to the lowering of inhibitions in the brain than to any direct effect on the digestive system—when the inhibitions go, so does the diet.

When alcohol depresses the brain, many of the bodily functions that are regulated by the brain are also impaired. For instance, alcohol throws off the body's water balance, which causes the kidneys to excrete excessive amounts of water. This imbalance explains part of the dehydration problem of hangovers.

An alcohol-drugged brain also results in a lack of motor skills and sensory perception while at the same time promoting a feeling of self-confidence and sociability. This combination of effects presents a number of problems in other areas of the body. As Shakespeare noted in Macbeth, "It provokes the desire, but it takes away the performance." Impaired sexual performance is only one ego-deflating response of the body to a sluggish brain.

The side effects of alcohol should pose no serious threat to the moderate drinker. In fact, some studies reveal that small quantities of alcohol may even be good for you; moderate amounts of red wine, for example, have been shown to be effective in helping to prevent certain types of heart disease. At any rate, moderate and responsible drinking generally will not lead to health problems.

ALCOHOLISM

The intermediate stage between socialism and capitalism is alcoholism.

—Norman Brenner

Once wrongly considered to be a weakness rather than a disease, alcoholism is still a somewhat mysterious illness. While an estimated 10.5 million people in the United States alone are alcoholics, alcoholism's causes are only partially understood. A variety of factors, both internal and external, have been linked to the development of the disease. The children of alcoholics are more likely than others to contract the disease; on the other hand, plenty of alcoholics have no family history of alcohol abuse. Certain personality traits—impulsivity, non-conformity, a sense of alienation—are shared by many alcoholics, yet it is unclear whether these are causes or merely symptoms of the disease. Emotional problems and stress can lead to substance abuse in almost any person; alcoholics frequently use liquor to mask emotional pain or negative feelings. Social acceptability also plays a distinct role. Many college students, for example, exhibit symptoms of alcoholism that disappear once they leave the beer-soaked hallways of undergraduate life.

Whatever its causes, there are a number of symptoms that point to alcoholism:

1. Occasional "binges"—periods of uncontrolled drinking.
2. Drinking in order to get drunk or an inability to stop at just one or two drinks.
3. An increasing tolerance to alcohol—using increasingly large quantities of alcohol to achieve the same effect.
4. Work- or school-related problems that are caused by drinking; personal problems caused by drinking.
5. Avoiding family or friends while drinking; irritation at any discussion of your drinking by family or friends.
6. Failure to keep promises to yourself about controlling or cutting down your drinking.
7. Feelings of guilt about drinking; frequent regret over things you have said or done when drunk.
8. Frequent blackouts.
9. Irregular eating habits during periods of heavy drinking.
10. Using alcohol as an escape from personal problems.

This is only a partial list, but it covers most of the bases. Number 4 is probably the most obvious symptom of alcoholism.

While its causes are unclear, the effects of alcoholism are well known. Alcohol abuse leads to a myriad of personal and professional problems: alcoholics frequently lose their jobs, friends, spouses, and children because of their inability to avoid regular heavy drinking. Suicide rates are also consistently high among alcoholics.

These emotional problems become compounded by the inevitable destruction of the chronic alcoholic's body. Physically addicted to liquor, chronic alcoholics often suffer delirium tremens (DTs) when withdrawing from alcohol without proper medical care. DTs involve three to six days of shaking, fever, acute panic, and vivid hallucinations. This experience sometimes frightens the problem drinker away from alcohol for a while, but, unfortunately, many eventually return to their previous condition.

After years of addiction, many chronic alcoholics virtually stop eating, as alcohol replaces the calories food once provided. Since alcohol has no nutritional value, most alcoholics develop serious vitamin and mineral deficiencies as well as diseases that accompany such malnutrition. Beriberi, a condition resulting from vitamin B shortages, often reveals itself in the alcoholic as Korsakoff's psychosis or Wernicke's syndrome, both characterized by gradual memory loss, confusion, and disorientation.

The liver, which plays such a large role in processing alcohol in the body, takes a tremendous beating. After just two days of heavy drinking, a person can develop fatty liver as the result of a breakdown in the mechanism that moves fat from the liver into the blood. Very long periods of drinking increase the severity of this condition, or may lead to alcoholic hepatitis and inflammation of the liver. Some alcoholics' livers become scarred and hardened from abuse. This condition, known as cirrhosis, is a leading cause of death in many areas of the country.

Long-term, heavy drinking may also lead to destruction within the digestive and circulatory systems. Many alcoholics develop chronic irritation of the stomach lining as the result of alcohol's constant stimulation of gastric fluids. Some contract cancer of the mouth, pharynx, larynx, or esophagus. After a long period of regularly taxing the heart, alcoholism may also give rise to heart diseases and an increased risk of high blood pressure.

Technically, alcoholism is incurable—complete abstinence allows alcoholics to lead normal lives, but most will never be able to enjoy even a social drink. Today, most rehabilitation programs revolve around detoxification. Medical professionals supervise the alcoholic's withdrawal, treat DT symptoms, provide medical care for physical ailments, and offer psychological guidance to ease the reformed alcoholic into a life of abstinence. Support groups such as Alcoholics Anonymous also help an alcoholic stay on the wagon.

Keep Them Doggies Rollin'

Contrary to popular belief, the association of sobriety with being "on the wagon" has nothing to do with a posse comitatus comprised of angry members of the temperance movement rounding up sods. Nor did the development of the phrase have anything to do with the disgruntled Irish who were forced aboard the "paddy wagon" in corrupt, late-18th century police sweeps of the city. It certainly was not the case that bandwagons—the bawdy circus wagons carrying musical bands—demonstrated any kind of admirable abstinence. Instead, in the days when them automated riding machines were but far-off dreams of the insane and when fillies and buggies ruled the world, horses would roam the unpaved cities pulling along water wagons, from which the "streets" would be showered in order to diminish the billowing dust clouds caused by traffic. Those who gave up alcohol—ostensibly to adopt water as their beverage of choice—were described as having "climbed aboard the water wagon," a phrase that was clipped to "on the wagon."

DRUNK DRIVING

Simply put, driving drunk is one of the dumbest things you can do. The facts speak for themselves—over 16,000 people were killed in the United States in 1997 in alcohol-related car accidents, while over a million people were injured. Damages from drunk driving accidents and associated legal, clinical, and other expenses amount to about $45 billion per year. And if this present trend continues, there is a 60% chance that you will be involved in an alcohol-related crash at some time in your life.

You don't need to be very drunk to cause an accident. At 0.05% BAC—only one or two drinks for some people—drivers lose inhibitions and feel more relaxed about everything. Someone at this level of intoxication might misjudge the severity of a driving situation and fail to recognize a potential accident until it's too late.

As the BAC increases, driver reflexes deteriorate. At 0.10% BAC, motor areas in the brain become depressed, resulting in slowed reaction times and uncoordinated movements. At this stage, drivers' reflexes may be too slow to respond to a hazardous situation even if they can recognize it.

At higher levels, coordination and judgment deteriorate even further. Drunk drivers also develop vision problems as alcohol affects the delicate muscle structure of the eye. With such poor powers of judgment, motor control, and eyesight, driving at this point is an invitation to tragedy.

The chart below shows the statistical relationship between BAC levels and automobile accidents. (The BAC information here and in the remainder of the section is courtesy of the Mothers Against Drunk Driving.)

BAC (%)	RISK OF ACCIDENT
0.05	2-3 times normal risk
0.08	5-6 times normal risk
0.10	7-8 times normal risk
0.15	300 times normal risk

Do you remember all those drunkenness variables—mood, metabolism, age, and so on—listed earlier in the chapter? Taking those into consideration, the figures in this chart reflect the lowest probability for an individual. If a driver feels tired, is on medication, has a slow metabolism, a weak liver, or maybe just had a rough day, the chances of accident could skyrocket.

What if you do drive and happen to get caught? The consequences depend on where you are at the time. In most states, holding a driver's license gives the authorities your "implied consent" to perform a Breathalyzer test and to require that you take it. If you refuse, you face prosecution.

The Breathalyzer measures your BAC level. In many states, a 0.10% BAC constitutes per-se evidence of driving under the influence of alcohol—that is, conclusive evidence that you were driving drunk. States with a per-se intoxication of 0.10% include: Alaska, Arizona, Arkansas,

Colorado, Connecticut, Delaware, District of Columbia, Georgia, Indiana, Iowa, Kentucky, Louisiana, Maryland, Michigan, Minnesota, Mississippi, Missouri, Montana, Nebraska, Nevada, New Jersey, New York, North Dakota, Ohio, Oklahoma, Pennsylvania, Rhode Island, South Dakota, Tennessee, Texas, Washington, West Virginia, Wisconsin, and Wyoming.

Through 1998, 15 states had passed legislation dropping the BAC level for a DUI charge to 0.08% (a policy that the U.S. Department of Transportation is trying to pass on the national level). These states include: Alabama, California, Florida, Hawaii, Idaho, Illinois, Kansas, Maine, New Hampshire, New Mexico, North Carolina, Oregon, Utah, Vermont, and Virginia.

Laws in Massachusetts and South Carolina are not per-se laws. A BAC of 0.10% (0.08% in Massachusetts) is evidence of alcohol impairment but isn't illegal per se.

In addition to these laws, every state except South Carolina, South Dakota, and Wyoming has laws on the books with different DUI levels for underage drinkers. Nine states—Arizona, Illinois, Maine, Michigan, North Carolina, Oklahoma, Oregon, Utah and Wisconsin—and the District of Columbia consider drivers under 21 with a BAC above 0.00% to be driving under the influence. California and New Jersey consider drivers under 21 with a 0.01% BAC to be driving under the influence. Alabama, Arkansas, Colorado, Connecticut, Delaware, Florida, Georgia, Idaho, Indiana, Iowa, Kansas, Kentucky, Louisiana, Maryland, Massachusetts, Minnesota, Mississippi, Montana, Nebraska, Nevada, New Hampshire, New Mexico, New York, North Dakota, Ohio, Pennsylvania, Rhode Island, Tennessee, Texas, Vermont, Virginia, Washington, and West Virginia all prohibit drivers under 21 from driving with a BAC in excess of 0.02% (Hawaii has a 0.02% BAC for drivers under 18). Mississippi considers drivers under 21 with a BAC of 0.08% to be under the influence.

Don't trust these lists for too long, however—the laws are constantly changing, usually in the direction of stricter legislation against drunk driving. Anyway, unless you go to a bar with a Breathalyzer, there's no sure way to measure your BAC. The safest way to protect yourself is to abstain from drinking before driving.

THE BARTENDER'S RESPONSIBILITIES

All of this information affects a bartender considerably. Since judgment is the first response to fade in a drinker's dwindling brain, the bartender sometimes plays an active role in identifying customers who are too drunk to drive or to manage themselves. Perhaps concern for your customer's safety and welfare might not be enough to make your self-interested personage go through the hassle of "shutting off" a drunk.

QUIZ NUMBER 2:

Q: COMMENT ALLEZ VOUS?

Q: HOW MANY FINGERS?

Q: DOG SALT?

It's a lot easier to go on serving intoxicated people to keep them quiet. If, however, someone you served gets into a drunk driving accident, the blood will fall on your hands, from both a personal and a legal point of view. Nationwide, the government and judicial system have been cracking down on drunk driving since the 1980s. On one hand, the crackdown centers on catching and punishing people who drive under the influence of alcohol. Many states have passed stricter laws to deal with these people, including mandatory jail terms in some instances. On the other hand, legislators have recently been coming to the realization that maybe they should go closer to the root of the problem: if people don't get drunk, they won't drive drunk. After a certain point of lost judgment, however, a drinker cannot decide when to stop. Lawmakers would like to help these people by shifting the responsibility of judgment over to the people who serve liquor.

Dram shop legislation stems from this line of thought. Dram shop laws, statutes on the books of many states, make specific provisions, to prosecute the servers of drunks. If a person becomes intoxicated and causes damages, either the drunk or someone adversely affected by the drunk's actions can sue the establishment that served the liquor. It is not preserved solely for bars, either. Hosts of private parties have been held liable for damage caused by intoxicated guests.

Many states without dram shop statutes have prosecuted servers of drunks through case law. Suits against bar owners and party hosts established precedents of prosecution for similar subsequent cases.

These laws are getting tougher. In many states, the operator's license may be automatically revoked. Additionally, the bartenders themselves can be charged with a felony for intoxicating patrons. The consequences are rather drastic, since a felony can pop your ass in jail; even without hard time, a conviction on one's criminal record generally ruins the credit rating of offenders while also excluding them from such important activities as their ability to remain in their profession and their right to vote. Be forewarned.

How can you protect yourself, your patron, and the bar where you work? For starters, read this chapter carefully to learn how to recognize an intoxicated person. Some bars provide weight tables to help you decide how much to serve a person, but their accuracy is diminished by the confluence of other factors governing one's state of drunkenness, so be careful. Also remember that your bar or party may not be a drinker's first stop of the evening, further compromising the utility of these charts. Recently, some bars have purchased Breathalyzers to help patrons decide when to stop drinking and/or to call a cab. Since their use remains voluntary, however, this method has not met great success, although it's a step in the right direction. To some degree, you can shield yourself and your bar of liability by fully documenting steps that you take to prevent a drunken patron from causing harm (many bars have a journal in which you can enter relevant observations of this nature).

If a person shows signs of intoxication, do not serve that person. Then again, some drinkers can go all night without so much as a slur...but they might get behind the wheel and lose control. To prevent such problems, try to keep track of your customers and don't serve anyone too much, regardless of outward appearances. Unfortunately, this is easier said than done, as many drinkers become belligerent in the face of such humiliation. To avoid unpleasant situations, be very discreet; quietly refuse to serve alcohol, then offer the guest some soda or coffee—or better yet, water. With a non-alcoholic drink, the patron probably won't feel so embarrassed about being shut off, and it's very difficult for anyone to refuse the offer of a free beverage. If the customer appears to be dangerously drunk, quietly offer to call a cab. Some people will appreciate your kindness and sensitivity. Some will call you names that would normally merit washing their mouths with soap. If a patron sets off fireworks at the suggestion of a shut-off, you may have to become more forceful; summon the manager to help you and, if necessary, the police as well. Despite the hassle it might cause you at the time, your responsible, alert attitude toward intoxicated people will probably spare everybody much greater problems later.

There are other, more creative ways of dealing with drunks that some bartenders feel more comfortable employing, all of which are non-confrontational (the last thing in the world that you want to do is to provoke someone who is intoxicated). Effective server responses include first-person sob stories, such as stating that you're concerned about the drinker's safety, or that you could lose your job if you continue serving the patron. Offers of freebies also help—either provide a drinker with some complimentary food or a free, non-alcoholic beverage. At the very least, these actions will slow down the consumption of alcohol, and stalling can be one of the most effective and non-confrontational approaches to deal with potential problem drinkers.

Minors pose another problem. If caught serving underage people, a bar might automatically have its license suspended or revoked and be forced to pay hefty fines. Do not serve alcohol to those under 21. Ask for positive identification from all suspected underagers and refuse service if they cannot produce it. When you examine an I.D., don't just look at the birth year; also check the birth date, since it remains illegal to sell liquor to someone who is but two days shy of her magical 21st. Also check the expiration date of the I.D., and if there's some doubt about whether or not the person depicted truly owns the I.D., line up the skeletal structure of the face in a straight line going down from the forehead to the nose to the chin.

There are training courses in alcohol safety that provide a much more exhaustive outline of effective server responses and appropriate actions to undertake as a bartender. While any aspiring bartenders are well served to take such a strategy course, some cities, counties, and states actually require prospective bartenders to take some kind of safety certification class. The TIPS (Training for Intervention ProcedureS) class is the most widespread of them—ask bartenders in your area if you are required to take one. Alcohol servers, after all, must experience their own ivory towers.

FOR MORE ON BARTENDING SAFETY

The TIPS program offers an excellent website with detailed information about state-by-state liquor (and bartending) laws, while also offering a full list of TIPS programs available in your region. Visit them at http://www.gettips.com, or contact them by phone at 1-800-GETTIPS/438-8477. Mothers Against Drunk Driving also offers a detailed website that discusses laws and regulations as well as prevention and treatment measures for alcoholism and alcohol safety at http://www.madd.org. The National Highway Traffic Safety Administration explores trends and developments in laws related to drinking and serving alcohol (http://www.nhtsa.dot.gov).

APPENDIX

APPENDIX

Bartenders (and drinkers) love to throw around jargon to make their jobs or lives sound more interesting than they really are, but some of the following words are indispensable for communicating exactly what you want to order or mix.

TERMINOLOGY

PROOF: Proof is twice the percentage of alcohol. For example, 100 proof equals 50% alcohol. This term indicates the strength of the liquor. The proof of a drink may range from 0 to 200, with most alcohols in mixed drinks being about 80 proof, the average wine around 15 proof, and the average beer running about 8 proof. These numbers are only rough guidelines; the actual proof of a liquor is usually listed on the label.

GRAIN NEUTRAL SPIRITS (GNS): This 190-proof (95% pure) alcohol has no distinctive color, odor, or taste. Both vodka and gin are initially prepared as GNS and then later filtered or flavored and cut with distilled water. In some states it is possible to buy grain in liquor stores; if you plunge forth and purchase it, be careful! One grain drink is as intoxicating as three to four ordinary drinks, yet no flavor, color, or odor signals this potency to the drinkers. GNS is very irritating to the throat and should never be consumed straight. Everclear is the most common brand name for GNS.

NEAT: Alcohol served right from the bottle with no ice.

STRAIGHT UP: A drink mixed in a glass with ice and then strained into another glass without ice (sometimes referred to as a chilled drink).

ON THE ROCKS: Refers to a drink with ice. In some cases the drink is prepared as a straight-up drink, but is then strained into a rocks glass with ice.

SIDE/BACK/CHASER: Some bars, instead of regular highballs, serve a glass of mixer with 1½ oz. of liquor on the side in a shot glass. This glass of mixer is called a side, back, or chaser.

MIST/FRAPPÉ: Both terms refer to a drink served over shaved ice, but a mist is generally served in a rocks glass and a frappé in a cocktail or champagne glass. For example, a "Crème de Menthe

Mist" describes crème de menthe poured over shaved ice in a rocks glass.

DRY/SWEET: Refers to the proportion of vermouth in a martini and the kind of vermouth in a Manhattan. (See pages 57-64.)

STRAIGHT/BLENDED/MALTED: These terms refer to whiskey. (See page 20-22.)

LABELING: The letters on a brandy or whiskey bottle describe the contents. They are usually listed in combination. For example, VSOP on a brandy label stands for Very Special Old Pale. These letters are primarily used in descriptive fashion, but they should give you some idea of the quality of the liquor.

> C—cognac or Canadian
> E—especially
> F—fine
> M—mellow
> O—old
> P—pale
> Q—quart
> S—special or superior
> V—very
> X—extra

VIRGIN: A drink prepared without liquor—for example, a Virgin Mary (a Bloody Mary without vodka). For a selection of non-alcoholic drinks, see pages 140-142.

FRONT BAR: The area of the bar in which the most frequently used liquors and mixers (vodka, gin, rum, tequila, triple sec, vermouth, Rose's Lime Juice, Scotch, bourbon, and whiskey) are held. Also known as the well or cocktail party bar.

BACK BAR: Home to liqueurs, brandies, and less-frequently ordered alcohols. Also known as the liqueur bar.

HOUSE BRANDS: The default brands of alcohol used for making cocktails, the house brands are the ones that sit on the front bar.

CALL BRANDS: A step up from house brands, call brands must be ordered by name.

PREMIUM BRANDS: Top-notch liquor that won't make you sicker.

SODA GUN: A force for good struggling against the evil world of bottled mixers, a soda gun allows you to dispense of mixers with the mere touch of a button.

JUICERS: The plastic containers in which mixing juices are kept; they are known as store-and-pours among bartenders in the know, since they're transforming top allows them to either seal off juice from the menacing air or to pour the juice out through a nozzle.

ETHANOL: Also known as ethyl alcohol, it's the stuff you can drink and from which one can procure a buzz. Its sinister siblings, methyl and isopropyl alcohol, might give you a buzz, but they might also blind or kill you in the process.

DISTILLATION: The process of altering a substance by heating it, it is a method used to produce hard liquor.

HARVARD BARTENDING KIT: An absolutely indispensable tool in becoming a masterful mixologist. Buy one—today!

MEASUREMENTS

DASH/SPLASH: This refers to the amount of something in a drink, such as a dash of Tabasco sauce or a splash of water. Technically, a dash equals one-sixth of a teaspoon (in more precise terms, a few drops), while a splash equals a half-ounce (a long squirt), but a bartender very rarely measures these small amounts.

SHOT: A shot is no precise amount; it usually ranges from 1 to 3 oz. depending on the bar and the size of its shot glasses. A shot is also a type of drink.

JIGGER: 1½ oz.

PONY: 1 oz.

NIP: Nips are little bottles of liquor, popular as gifts at holiday time and as drink servings on airplanes, where they are also called miniatures. (Nips are given as gifts. People travel on airplanes around the holiday season, where they serve nips. People give gifts around the holidays. Very suspicious, no?) They come in three sizes: 1, 1.6, and 2 oz.

FIFTH: The traditional size of the American liquor bottle, now largely superseded by the 750 mL bottle. One-fifth of a gallon equals four-fifths of a quart or 25.6 oz.

KEG (technically, a half-keg): A stainless-steel beer barrel holding 15½ gallons.

Most distillers and wine makers now use metric measurements, paying little heed to the fact that the metric system is tearing America apart. This list illustrates the relationship between standard and metric amounts.

STANDARD	METRIC
1 pint = 16 ounces (oz.)	500 milliliters (mL) = 16.9 oz.
1 fifth = 25.6 oz.	750 mL = 25.4 oz.
1 quart = 32 oz.	1 liter (L) = 33.8 oz.

Other terms of the art in reference to bottles can get a little bit fanciful (though they are actually real, standard sizes): the Magnum (52 oz.), the Jeroboam (104 oz.), the Rehoboam (156 oz.), the Methuselah (208 oz.), the Salmanazar (312 oz.), the Balthazar (416 oz.) and finally, the Nebuchadnezzar (clocking in at an amazing 520 oz.–the equivalent of 20 "normal" bottles of champagne). The last terms are seldom used, since people can't lift some of these ridiculously large bottles, let alone hoist them skyward for the purposes of pouring them. But, as an aside, a 1.5-meter-tall sherry bottle was blown in Stafford-shire, England, in 1958. It holds about 26 gallons (3328 oz.) or a little over 6.5 Nebuchadnezzars. They decided to call it an Adelaide. Twenty six gallons of wine would weigh around 220 pounds–not including all that glass, of course. You may never see or hear them again, and it can be said with some confidence that you will never witness anyone drinking them from a brown paper bag.

FOR THOSE WHO ALWAYS WANT MORE

A few websites have virtually mastered mixology, and those who want to find more information on that obscure drink would be well-served to consult them for those improbable bits of information that slipped through the cracks of this tome.

www.webtender.com: An outstanding site that allows you to find the recipes of a ridiculously large number of drinks. Alternatively, the site spits out a list of all known concoctions that can be produced with the ingredients of your choice.

www.ozemail.com.au/~berghous/drink.html: A clever product from the country that brought you kangaroos, this site goes into excellent detail about the specifics of obscure liqueurs. They also offer a recipe of the week for those looking to expand their drink lexicon at a reasonable pace.

www.TheVirtualBar.com: Virtual bar indeed...from the on-line jukebox to the secrets of professional bartenders to the dizzying collection of recipes down to the games, a visit to this site almost merits a line on the resume of an aspiring bartender.

www.food.epicurious.com/d_drinking/d00_home/drinking.html: A somewhat more nuanced approach that rounds out its drink recipes with some fine suggestions for the use of alcohol in cooking. Thoughtful articles and an excellent dictionary of wines contribute to the sense of refinement.

www.gettips.com: An important resource for the careful bartender, this website details state-by-state liquor laws and also provides information on their courses on bartending safety.

www.madd.org: Another important collection focusing and regulations and safety tactics.

INDEX

T

W

Y

Z

OFFICIAL BARTENDER'S PAD
USE ONLY FOR APPLICABLE RECIPES AND NOTES

STANDARD	METRIC
1 pint = 16 ounces (oz.)	500 milliliters (mL) = 16.9 oz.
1 fifth = 25.6 oz.	750 mL = 25.4 oz.
1 quart = 32 oz.	1 liter (L) = 33.8 oz.

OFFICIAL BARTENDER'S PAD
USE ONLY FOR APPLICABLE RECIPES AND NOTES

STANDARD	METRIC
1 pint = 16 ounces (oz.)	500 milliliters (mL) = 16.9 oz.
1 fifth = 25.6 oz.	750 mL = 25.4 oz.
1 quart = 32 oz.	1 liter (L) = 33.8 oz.

OFFICIAL BARTENDER'S PAD
USE ONLY FOR APPLICABLE RECIPES AND NOTES

STANDARD	METRIC
1 pint = 16 ounces (oz.)	500 milliliters (mL) = 16.9 oz.
1 fifth = 25.6 oz.	750 mL = 25.4 oz.
1 quart = 32 oz.	1 liter (L) = 33.8 oz.

OFFICIAL BARTENDER'S PAD
USE ONLY FOR APPLICABLE RECIPES AND NOTES

STANDARD	METRIC
1 pint = 16 ounces (oz.)	500 milliliters (mL) = 16.9 oz.
1 fifth = 25.6 oz.	750 mL = 25.4 oz.
1 quart = 32 oz.	1 liter (L) = 33.8 oz.

OFFICIAL BARTENDER'S PAD
USE ONLY FOR APPLICABLE RECIPES AND NOTES

STANDARD	METRIC
1 pint = 16 ounces (oz.)	500 milliliters (mL) = 16.9 oz.
1 fifth = 25.6 oz.	750 mL = 25.4 oz.
1 quart = 32 oz.	1 liter (L) = 33.8 oz.

OFFICIAL BARTENDER'S PAD
USE ONLY FOR APPLICABLE RECIPES AND NOTES

STANDARD	METRIC
1 pint = 16 ounces (oz.)	500 milliliters (mL) = 16.9 oz.
1 fifth = 25.6 oz.	750 mL = 25.4 oz.
1 quart = 32 oz.	1 liter (L) = 33.8 oz.

OFFICIAL BARTENDER'S PAD
USE ONLY FOR APPLICABLE RECIPES AND NOTES

STANDARD	METRIC
1 pint = 16 ounces (oz.)	500 milliliters (mL) = 16.9 oz.
1 fifth = 25.6 oz.	750 mL = 25.4 oz.
1 quart = 32 oz.	1 liter (L) = 33.8 oz.

OFFICIAL BARTENDER'S PAD
USE ONLY FOR APPLICABLE RECIPES AND NOTES

STANDARD	METRIC
1 pint = 16 ounces (oz.)	500 milliliters (mL) = 16.9 oz.
1 fifth = 25.6 oz.	750 mL = 25.4 oz.
1 quart = 32 oz.	1 liter (L) = 33.8 oz.

OFFICIAL BARTENDER'S PAD
USE ONLY FOR APPLICABLE RECIPES AND NOTES

STANDARD	METRIC
1 pint = 16 ounces (oz.)	500 milliliters (mL) = 16.9 oz.
1 fifth = 25.6 oz.	750 mL = 25.4 oz.
1 quart = 32 oz.	1 liter (L) = 33.8 oz.

OFFICIAL BARTENDER'S PAD
USE ONLY FOR APPLICABLE RECIPES AND NOTES

STANDARD	METRIC
1 pint = 16 ounces (oz.)	500 milliliters (mL) = 16.9 oz.
1 fifth = 25.6 oz.	750 mL = 25.4 oz.
1 quart = 32 oz.	1 liter (L) = 33.8 oz.

A. BARTENDING KIT

Comes with everything you need to be a successful bartender! Shaker, mixing glass, strainer, bar spoon, jigger/pony, corkscrew, and six speedpourers.

$39.95

B. EXTRA SPEEDPOURERS

For your expanding bar needs.

$4.95

PRICES SUBJECT TO CHANGE.

. . . .

ORDER FORM

ITEM	QTY	AMT
A. BARTENDING KIT: #35.95 plus $5.00 postage and han-dling. (Mass. residents add 5% sales tax)		
B. EXTRA SPEED-POURERS: $4.95 (Mass. residents add 5% sales tax)		

NAME_____

ADDRESS
(NO. & STREET) ——————————

CITY/STATE/ZIP _____

TELEPHONE ——————————

TOTAL _____

ENCLOSE A CHECK OR MONEY ORDER PAYABLE TO: HARVARD STUDENT AGENCIES, INC., 67 MOUNT AUBURN ST. CAMBRIDGE, MA 02138, (617) 495-3033